Tales of rambunctious adventure
in the famed

Columbia River Gorge

and along
the legendary

Columbia River Highway

HISTORIC
COLUMBIA
RIVER
HIGHWAY

To
Mr F Vey Parsons ~ —

The author hopes you may find
pleasure in perusing these
pages. This is mans effort to
portray something of the grandeur
and the glory of the Gorge of
the Columbia, where the
hand of God wrought mightily.

Samuel C. Lancaster
Portland Oregon
August 8th
1916

Inscription by Lancaster to a friend
in his 1915 book "The Columbia River Highway"

SAMUEL C. LANCASTER
1864 - 1941
CHIEF ENGINEER
SCENIC COLUMBIA RIVER HIGHWAY 1913 - 1915
PIONEER BUILDER OF HARD-SURFACE ROADS. HIS
GENIUS OVERCAME TREMENDOUS OBSTACLES,
EXTENDING AND REPLACING THE EARLY TRAIL
THROUGH THE COLUMBIA RIVER GORGE WITH A
HIGHWAY OF POETRY AND DRAMA SO THAT MILLIONS
COULD ENJOY GOD'S SPECTACULAR CREATIONS.

Samuel Christopher Lancaster
Visionary designer-engineer of the remarkable
Historic Columbia River Highway

Memorial is located at Vista House on the old highway.

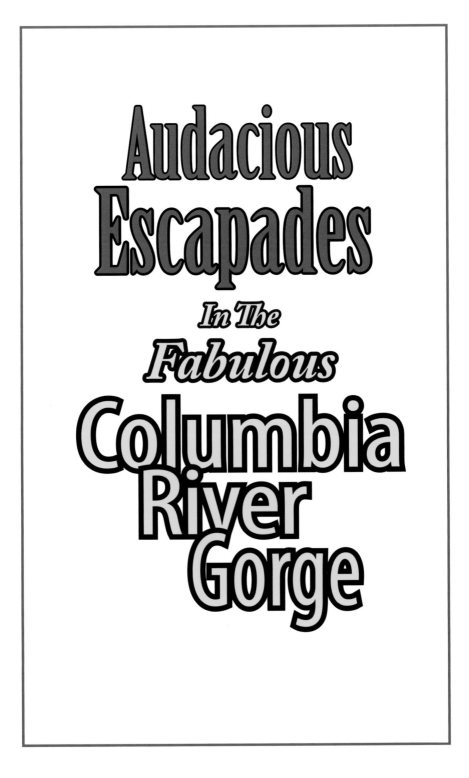

Audacious Escapades

In The Fabulous

Columbia River Gorge

Audacious Escapades
in the
Fabulous
Columbia River Gorge

COPYRIGHT © 2007 MARC PAULSEN PRESS

MARC PAULSEN PRESS
19210 S.W. Martinazzi Avenue P.M.B. #817
Tualatin, Oregon 97062

503-330-1226

•

First Printing 2007

•

ISBN 0-9774737-1-6
ISBN13: 978-0-9774737-1-7

Marc Paulsen's adult background ranges from brickmason and masonry contracting to general construction contractor, advertising, interior design, event coordinating, equipment engineering, fine art sales, airplane sales and project manager for large sawmill installations. He has served on management assignments including trade show exhibitions of national scope, high-rise office construction projects, electronics installations and museum consultant.

From early experiences as a thirteen-year-old hitchhiker on the historic old Columbia River Highway to hopping freight trains and sleeping in "hobo jungles," Marc Paulsen's life has been one long series of unique adventures. His pursuits have included hot-rodding, auto and motorcycle racing, parachuting, biplane aerobatics and collecting and dealing in antique autos and rare books. He has traveled many countries and while serving with the U.S. Armed Forces in Europe, wrote numerous articles on tourism.

So that the reader doesn't conclude his life works were all smashing successes, it is worth knowing that, of the approximately eighty-seven paid endeavors in which Marc has engaged since age 9, he openly admits that many did not move far beyond "pass go." However, *educational and broadening*, they were!

Marc has had a lifelong infatuation with the marvelous Gorge of the Columbia River, partly from many unique experiences on and near the old highway and also from his belief that the Columbia Gorge ranks among the world's natural wonders. After countless trips through the Gorge covering 6 decades, he is still awestruck each repeat trip. May you enjoy Marc's tales of youthful exuberance and humorous escapades...and allow a bit of charity in your judgments.

Crystaline water along the
Historic Columbia River Highway

Contents

The Columbia
America's Great
Highway

From Samuel Lancaster's 1915 book that tells the story
of the great highway's design and construction

Introduction

"There is a time and a place for every man
to act his part in life's drama
and to build according to his ideals."

Samuel Christopher Lancaster
Designer-Engineer, Columbia River Highway

From its opening on July 6, 1915, first-time tourists unfailingly found the remarkable old Columbia River Highway awe-inspiring. To me, at age eleven, the highway's magnificence in beauty and construction struck indelible memories.

This book's frontispiece is a reproduction of designer Lancaster's lovingly created inscription to a friend. A supremely elegant execution of hand-calligraphy, he placed it in a 1916 edition of his detailed book telling his Columbia River Highway story. His superb hand lettering and the majestic highway he designed are one and the same in supremacy–masterpieces of artistic design and engineering. Even now, it is impossible to drive the few existing old highway sections without a warm feeling that one is rolling along cradled in the arms of this eminent design master. The highway and his brilliant plan for an artful Crown Point rest station enroute were so grandiose that it was as if Lancaster had borrowed concepts from the art world's old masters. *They were that good!*

Remarkably, *two* "Sams" were inspirational in man's creations in the Gorge: Samuel Hill (son of James Hill, builder of the Great Northern Railroad) who promoted the idea of building and improving many road systems in the northwest and Samuel Lancaster, the

1

Vista House on Crown Point in spectacular Columbia Gorge–
Lancaster's majestic inspiration for a viewpoint

principal designer and construction engineer.

Hill and Lancaster visited Europe and, after viewing highways in the Swiss Alps, Hill suggested the possibility of a similar highway through the Columbia Gorge. Lancaster then provided the artistic design and engineering expertise to build it.

My own enchantment with the highway carried to my military obligation in Germany. Homesick servicemen the world over post photos in their wall lockers. My *most important* photo was of Crown Point and Vista House taken years ago from Chanticleer Point. *That is affection!*

I've had many truly unique experiences involving the highway: some inspirational, some dangerous, some great sport and a few plain hilarious.

My first tour was movingly "inspirational." It was during World War II when gas was "rationed" and the speed limit was 35 miles per hour. Simply accumulating enough gasoline to drive without harming the "war effort" was touchy. We motored the heights to Vista House and marveled at the expansive view. "Awe" is the best description of our reaction to Lancaster's superb staging of the location.

Following are some of my wilder adventures on the old road which will have to be chalked up to youthful exuberance and the reader must understand that I am a reformed man!

Western view from Vista House

Vista House information desk

Architectural detail of octagonal structure

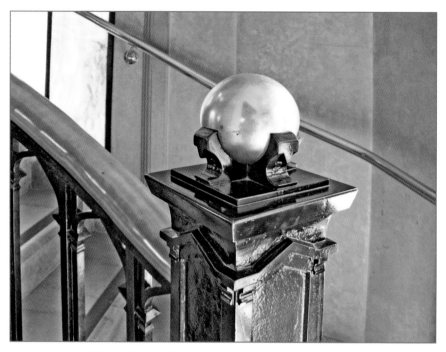

Newell post decoration - balcony stairway

Visitors read Lancaster tribute

Author...age 17

Maybe The Moose Had It Right

Young men are not much different from Bull Moose when it comes to impressing the ladies. The Bull Moose does it by bashing heck out of all competition that gets anywhere close to sniffing distance. Teen-age boys have a number of devices in their arsenals to achieve the same goal.

I'd been trying like crazy to impress a girl who had me "smitten" to the core. This required wowing her with a man-of-the-world, strong-guy, can-do approach.

It was hard to believe my good fortune when she thought me adequate for consideration. This had the makings of the big one! Of course, first she had to be convinced beyond all question that I was the number one "Bull of the Woods."

If a boy lives "high on the hill" and his family has means, he can simply show up in a fancy automobile with a bundle of cash in his pocket and wow the gal with upscale goodies and costly activities. A moose would probably do that, too, if he could drive a car and figure out how to count bills and make change. It would be a heck of a lot simpler than risking banged-up antlers. If you come from more modest circumstances as I did, it is necessary to be much more inventive.

So…enter my brand new (to me) used motorcycle. My purchase had been based largely on the amount of noise it made. This in a time when, if you were really "with it," you would have "megaphone" tailpipes…and man, this baby had them in spades. Giant double chrome funnels pointed backward. You could hear it coming within a two-mile radius!

This gal needed to be amazed by my riding expertise on this fabulous decibel-generator. That most certainly would endear me to her and we would live happily ever after—riding off into the sunset and breaking sound-level records every mile of the way!

A grand sunny day found us thundering up the old Columbia River Highway…with her fancy little bottom planted squarely on my "buddy seat" and snuggled up against me.

We wheeled up the highway…first to Chanticleer Point to check the view and then on to good old Vista House where we pulled into a space overlooking the river. We gazed at the fantastic views for a while (as long as I could stand it…something like five anxious minutes). Telling her of a unique activity I had lined up and ready for action, we then zinged downhill headed for the new highway at Lower Corbett.

A couple of weeks earlier, a beckoning hill on the highway had intrigued me. It appeared suitable for motorcycle "hill-climbing" practice…although that was something I'd not yet attempted. The plan was simple: demonstrate fantastic riding ability by zooming up the steep hill as she observed my expertise, hopefully with unmitigated admiration!

Earlier, after talking to motorcyclists who had done hill-climbing, it seemed clear that it was not complicated. Visualizing the grand possibilities of impressing this neat little gal, I pulled up short at the bottom of the hill. My future bride, a little perplexed…innocently inquired, "Why are we stopping here? I thought we going up to Multnomah Falls."

"Well, this is a good hill to demonstrate what these 'English bikes' can do." Then I explained the intricacies of motorcycle "hill-climbing" and told her she now was going to get a demonstration. It was my presumption that she would be so taken with the astonishing vision of me rocketing up this steep hill that she would be impressed forever. After suggesting to her a good position for viewing the action, she hiked halfway up the hill and placed herself so she could get the full effect of my booming race to the top.

The incline that gave me an unforgettable experience in motorcycle hill-climbing

When she seemed properly positioned to admire my raw courage, I aimed the bike toward a level bare patch of grass at the top of the hill just in front of dense trees and brush. Twisting the throttle a few times for ultimate effect produced a deafening roar that she surely would associate with a legendary man like James Bond...or maybe even Mr. Universe on wheels!

With my heart pounding from both wishful thoughts of a newly captured love and the nervous knowledge that I didn't know what in hell I was doing...the clutch was dropped...and the bike blasted off! The machine shot up the steep hill past her at about forty miles an hour gaining speed by the nanosecond.

Then...*everything went blank!*

Oh yes...the top of the hill *was reached.*

In fact, it was reached at about sixty miles an hour! That was the

9

precise moment when the throttle stuck…*wide open!*

Regaining my consciousness about ten minutes later…this fabulous new girlfriend was holding my head…but not appearing very sympathetic.

"What happened?"

"I don't know," she replied as she slapped at her legs…now viciously punctured by thousands of horribly irritating and painful fresh green nettles of spring. "You just shot off through the brush and disappeared."

Because she thought me injured or dead…she had rushed to the aid of this idiot…through an almost impenetrable jungle of nettles.

The good news? My body wasn't permanently damaged. The bad news? We both were riddled with the most god-awful cases of nettles imaginable…and now had to face even more of the nasty little needles simply to escape this ugly situation.

There was not much point in trying to explain. We now had to figure how to get our mode of transportation back down on the highway. The bike and I had continued *over* the top of the hill…then angled down the backside *more than a hundred yards* and crashed through dense underbrush before coming to rest with the machine on top of me! The brush was as thick as a rainforest and solidly interspersed with six-foot high nettles.

The upshot?

After working like dogs for over two hours in the wickedly thick nettles and heavy brush to get the bike back up to the hilltop, *then* down to the highway, she somehow mysteriously had lost interest in me. She didn't say a word on the way back to town…all the while rubbing her legs furiously in an attempt to neutralize the vicious stinging of the nettle barbs.

At her house, we mumbled abbreviated goodbyes…and my technicolor dreams of flowering romance faded to black and white as her home disappeared into the distance behind my roaring megaphone pipes.

Old highway switchbacks presented lurking danger.

On this one at Hood River, my motorcycle slid out from under me and crashed when 100° degree summer heat caused hot macadam tar to flow down the curve like warm molasses. It was necessary to leave the damaged machine behind and hitchhike the curvy highway home for help to retrieve it later.

The old highway saw fancy autos in the 1930s.

Troutdale now is an upscale destination for shoppers.

Railroad musem at Troutdale

Troutdale

Where the old Columbia River Highway begins
(Cabin living and dipping smelt)

1912 bridge over Sandy River at Troutdale...
Entrance to the Historic Columbia River Highway

In my young life, Troutdale, Oregon, played much more than being western gateway to the old Columbia River Highway. When our parents moved our family to Oregon from Iowa in June, 1942, that summer we had a Troutdale address. Our father, a bricklayer, landed a job helping build the giant Reynolds Metals Company aluminum plant a mile from the village. The plant produced lightweight metal for the tens of thousands of combat airplanes built during World War II. Because the "war effort" pinched housing availability to al-

Location beneath Sandy River bridge where commercial "dip-netters" harvested smelt fish by the multi-millions

most non-existence, upon arrival our family patriotically took the only thing then immediately available. Few people have lived in a "berry cabin," but we did! At that time, a major amount of the farmland around Portland was planted in strawberries, raspberries, boysenberries, blackberries and blackcaps (the latter, a berry then commandeered by the military for ink to stencil identification on millions of uniforms and other gear).

My father, mother, two sisters and I all lived for the summer strawberry season in two tiny primitive one-room structures. Most of the larger berry growers provided groups of cabins for "itinerant" berry pickers who were mostly poor people who did seasonal farm work and came from California and other areas. Many had arrived in California after leaving the mid-south during the deep depres-

14

sion of the early 30s. Others followed in the later 30s to escape the ruinous dust-storm era when topsoils literally blew away. To aid the "war effort," people (including young children) from all walks of life "pitched in" or were recruited to help with the harvests. We picked strawberries for one and one quarter cents per pound...plus a quarter cent per pound "bonus" for working through the entire summer berry season.

With crystal clarity, I remember little Troutdale because it had a "wool-pullery" nearby for processing sheepskin and it stank to high heaven. The odor carried for miles and it's a wonder the residents endured it. Fortunately, our cabins were beyond the fumes.

By summer's end, my folks' housing search turned up a small rental house (a wartime conversion from a large chicken-raising building). Its composition siding simulated brick. We lived there for the "duration" of the war when we were able to find and buy a house with acreage.

What is now the "Port of Portland" airport at Troutdale began as

WWII "Jeep" can

an auxiliary military field. In 1942, my dad and I would drive to the airport to watch Curtiss P-40 "Warhawks" and P-39 Bell "Airacobra" fighter planes constantly flying in, out and over the local area. There were also many Fairchild PT-19 "Primary Trainers," Ryan PT-22s and BT-13 "Basic Trainers." Two things there left permanent memories with me: first, the magnificent roar of the powerful fighter plane engines and second... "Jeep cans" full of aviation fuel stacked by the multi-thousands along the field. Apparently, there was a tank truck shortage.

A mile from Troutdale, the picturesque Sandy River meets "The Mighty Columbia." The Sandy was first named "Baring's River" by a George Vancouver expedition in 1792. In November 1805, Lewis and Clark called it the "Quicksand River" when they camped overnight near

Marc Paulsen Sr. with skiff used for Columbia River fishing and occasional waterfowl "jump-shooting"

Hunting/gathering runs in the family...
author's mother with prize Columbia River
salmon catch - 45 & 52 lbs.

its confluence with the Columbia. Later, by common usage, it became known as "Sandy River."

A major annual event on the Sandy River in Troutdale was "smelt dipping." Smelt are small silvery fish that average about seven to eight inches in length. The fish appeared in the early spring. This was big sport (and a source of extra food for many) during the 1940s and ran well into the 50s and 60s. The Sandy is bridged at the very beginning of the old Columbia River Highway and we used to "dip" for smelt right under that bridge. The "run" sometimes continued for days. People living near the bridge capitalized by renting out "dipping" nets. Cars would be parked for a half-mile and more in all directions from the action. There was no "limit" and one could haul away as many fish as one wished! Many people drove home with multiple washtubs full. Space directly beneath the bridge was usually reserved for "commercial" dippers who would tie up two or three large flat barges. They would bring fish up in massive quantities sometimes setting up generators and lights and dipping all night.

One of my first "wild" adventures on the historic Columbia River Highway took place at age thirteen during a smelt run. A school chum of mine actually owned a 1924 Model T Ford coupe. Yep! At thirteen! He had purchased it for five dollars. It had a few parts missing: the engine cover, the deck lid, some floorboards, the windshield and part of the roof. But, after much tinkering, it ran!

Our plan was to drive it down dangerously steep curvy roads necessary to get to the smelt dipping far below. We didn't worry about "little" details like driver's and car licenses.

The day we were ready to roll, the steering wheel either was misplaced or someone played a trick and made it disappear. Could've been his folks or a joker. He didn't slow down for even a minute. He beamed, "Heck, Marc…we'll just clamp a pair of "Vise-Grips™" on the steering wheel shaft…and we'll have it made." Riding with him steering desperately with a pair of "gripping" pliers as we wheeled down steep hills was the most hair-raising trip I have ever made to the old Columbia River Highway. We made it down and back… running off the road only once when the tool slipped off the splines on the steering wheel column. I've always felt my friend should have received some kind of award from the tool company for the most unique application of their highly useful product.

Commercial "dip-netters" worked all night to fill barges with smelt... directly beneath the old Troutdale Sandy River bridge.

For people of moderate means, the fish meant inexpensive meals. My mother prepared the little smelt fish simply by buttering a pan and plopping them into it. No cleaning required! We did that...*as we ate them.*

For reasons known only to the gods of nature, the massive smelt runs later dwindled and then disappeared completely. While they lasted, those amazing runs of fish allowed many to harvest useful free bounties...at the very head of the Historic Columbia River Highway.

"Caviar carriers" from the Columbia River...about 1910

Check the size of those sturgeon! In the early 1900s, when there was much wild "game" to be found in and near the Columbia River, this was the type of catch one could expect on a good day. When visiting Bonneville, John Day and McNary dams, it is still possible to observe fisherman hauling out giant sturgeon. Occasionally, fish as long as twelve feet and more are reeled in. Laws now protect the giant fish and they must be returned to the river...allowing continued regeneration of the species.

Classic design on the old highway

Oregon Trail "marker" located at
east end of Sandy River bridge

Stone masonry guardrails added an additional artistic touch
to many sections of the old highway.

21

View upriver from Chanticleer Point
Vista House can be spotted on top of lower cliff right of center.

Rooster Rock State Park is located on river in center of photo.
(Author waterskied there as member of "*Sons Of Beaches*" Waterski Club.)

In the nineteen forties and fifties (well before serious environmentalism), this location was a perfect place to practice marksmanship with shotguns. We teenagers would arrive with "clay" pigeons, "hand" target tossers, shotguns, a modest measure of 3.2% beer and shotgun shells to last a couple of hours. Happily blasting away, we would toss hundreds of clay pigeons aimed directly toward Vista House. The ones we hit went to their fragmented doom in the forest far below. The "good news?" Those "dead" clay pigeons have long ago worked their way deep into vegetation humus. Attempting this activity today, the long arm of the law would be minutes away and the penalty likely would be confiscation of guns, clays, shells, beer and automobiles and maybe...*us!*

Vista House on Crown Point attracts visitors by the thousands.
- 1918 -

Yellow and Black

Skinny and fat.

An interesting combination.

Why in the world would he be skinny and she fat? My gosh…she was his mother. Wouldn't he be fat, too? Nope! Didn't work that way. He was skinny as a rail!

School bored me and it wasn't possible to stay at home without being forced back to school. The result was my embarking on occasional "excursions." Some called it "running away." My preferred explanation was "adventure." Try hitchhiking from home with only thirty cents in your pocket and planning to be away for days or weeks at a time. *That's adventure!*

23

At the edge of a small high-desert Oregon village, I was thumbing my way back home from one such expedition. The array of passing vehicles included mostly locals: a lot of beat-up pickups, some big farm trucks and a few cars with ruddy farmer-types at the wheel. A couple of big diesel highway-rigs passed by with "No Riders" decals displayed prominently on their windshields. Passing next were a gasoline tanker of the type which never took riders and a couple of women drivers. It didn't look promising.

Then…a big Cadillac sedan pulling an enclosed trailer approached. Displaying a garish bright yellow auto body with black fenders, it was a sight to behold. But...pulling a trailer? And I'll be darned. *It stopped!*

Loping to the car, I peered in. Behind the wheel was a considerably hefty woman of about forty wearing a crazily-printed multicolored dress. A giant wide-brimmed woven straw hat was perched on her sizable head. If that wasn't shock enough, sitting in the back seat directly to her right was a tall skinny-as-a-rail pimply boy.

"What the heck is this?" went through my mind...and, "Why wasn't he sitting with her?"

"Hi," blurted from my gaping mouth.

"Hello there young man…get in," the woman firmly and loudly commanded as if she were a sergeant addressing a private. This setup looked screwy to me and my reaction was to step back a bit.

"Uhhhh….where are you going?" I queried. It seemed a good idea to check these two out more closely before committing. I hadn't often seen a goofier looking pair.

"We're going all the way to Gresham," she returned, "Get in."

"Uhhhh….you're going to Gresham?"

"Yes, get in!" she barked again.

"Uhhhh…."

Gresham was *my home!* Getting hooked up with this odd pair for such a long ride might be a mistake.

"Well, are you going to get in?"

"Uhhhh."

"Come along now, we're on a schedule."

"A schedule?"

"Yes…*a schedule!*"

"Uhhhh……well…..uhhhh….."

"Let's go…get in!" she again urged. "Are you going to get in?" she repeated once more, this time sounding more impatient.

Needing the ride, I thought, "What the heck, how bad can it be?" then opened the door and slid into the front seat next to the bulky woman.

"Well now, that's better," she blew over at me. "Where you going?"

Still in a state of shock over the appearance of this bizarre twosome, my thinking wasn't fast enough to hedge.

"Gresham."

"Why, that's just wonderful!" she puffed. "We'll look forward to seeing you there."

What that meant was anybody's guess but, with that, she immediately punched the car in gear like a truck driver, mashed the accelerator and we roared out of town. It was obvious she had done one heck of a lot of open-road driving.

Whipping along on the high desert straightaway, she began a quiz.

"Whatcha doing on the road?"

"Heading home."

"Where ya been?"

"Down south."

"Why aren't you in school?"

"Been visiting," I lied.

She abruptly changed the subject.

"*Do you know Jesus?*"

"Ohmigosh," *religion!*

"*Do you know Jesus?*" she repeated as if there were no choice but to answer.

"Uhhhh…well, maybe a little bit"…my answer hedged.

"You either know Jesus or you don't know Jesus," she persisted.

Turning my head to look back at the skinny kid, I wondered, "Did he know Jesus?" What the heck was this?

"Uhhhh…well, I've been to church."

"Yes, but do you know Jesus?"

This lady didn't give up. "Uhhh….what do you mean?"

One of America's most magnificent natural sights
...just minutes from Portland, Oregon

Multnomah Falls Lodge receives large crowds of visitors.

Multnomah Falls
620 total feet of clear water...located on the old highway
parallel with Interstate Hwy I-84

"Do you know Jesus…*have you been saved?*"

"Uhhhh…saved?"

"Yeah, 'saved.'"

"Golly, don't know…maybe."

"You'd know if you've been saved," she charged!

"Oh."

Fortunately, a giant truck was headed right at us and she backed off for a while to steer clear. As she tightened her grip on the wheel, I mentally wiped a bunch of perspiration. Boy, that had been close! Happily, the passing truck took her mind off the quiz-quest and she changed the Jesus subject for a while. Then she talked about this and that as we rolled along at high speed. Whatever it was she did, she sure knew how to drive! Then the respite ended.

"Sonny and me are going to hold a revival in Gresham. We just held one in Bend." She looked over at me and smiled sweetly through crooked teeth. "We're going to drive all the way around through the Columbia Gorge to get there. We've never been on that road and folks up here have been telling us it's a wonderful drive."

I almost choked. The revival mention came through loud and clear…especially the part about going to Gresham. I lived there! It explained the big covered trailer she was pulling and took only an instant to figure out what was in it. It had to be her revival equipment.

"Yep, we're all set. It's going to be wonderful! The weather looks like it will be nice and the man who set it up told us we have a good location for our tent."

My next thought was, "What kind of dingbat is helping her on the other end?" She rattled away about this revival and that revival they had held here and there. Made me wonder if they got run out of town occasionally…or what? The kid was just as screwy as she was. He had a tinny, high-pitched, whiny-sounding voice and all the time chimed in with affirmatives on the end of her sentences…as though he were "amen-ing" her words. Holy Toledo…what a pair! Well, at least on the surface they seemed fairly harmless. Finally, as we neared our destination, she hit on me.

"You're coming to our revival, aren't you?" she demanded…as if giving me the ride had obligated me.

28

"Uhhhh…well…uhhhh…maybe," knowing full well I had absolutely no intention of getting anywhere within a country mile of her operation.

"We'll expect you. You'll really enjoy it. Sonny sings some really good old gospel songs and plays the guitar really good. We'd sure like you to come."

"Maybe"…was my purposely vague response.

"That's good. We'll expect to see you there." She took the "maybe" as an affirmative.

My thought was, "Yeah…in your dreams!"

Reaching the edge of town, I misled her saying that my home was nearby…simply to bail out of the car sooner and the sooner the better! As she stopped to let me out, she parted with "You come to our meeting now, *hear?*"

I was relieved to be clear of these "lunatic fringers." Listening to her religion for *over a hundred and fifty miles* had been too much. Not one of my better rides; however, they were an interesting study.

Later, thinking about her and the kid and their crazy setup, the thought occurred that it might be interesting to see exactly how the two of them could put together an entire revival…apparently mostly by themselves. So…why not attend…just for the heck of it?

They had pitched a big oval circus-type tent on a vacant lot next to the Buick dealership, an odd location off the beaten track. Obviously they had to take "pot-luck" for a place to set up. Their tent looked like it had been through the mill. It was patched everywhere. The gaudy yellow and black Cadillac was parked directly by the rear door of the tent…aimed away from it as if they were ready for a fast get away if run out of town.

Sneaking up to the side of the tent, I slowly worked my way around to an opening that allowed a peek in to check it out. It appeared they had borrowed a whole bunch of cheap picnic table benches. This was really a "hayshaker" operation. It did look like they had a fairly decent "take-apart" stage platform. At least it appeared big enough for the two key players. The kid was tuning up and an old geezer was hobbling around…and that was it. Where were all the people? Didn't it take people to make a revival? I lagged outside in case I changed my mind.

During the next hour (while the lady evangelist stalled) a few oddball-appearing folks showed up and were seated in a scattered array. They appeared to be from the bottom of the socio-economic stratum…poor and scraggly. It was way past the start-up time she had posted. Obviously, she was hoping more souls would appear. They didn't. She had to go with eleven plus the geezer. Deciding to give it a shot, I slipped in quietly and sat behind the biggest guy who might hide me. This old gal had eyes like an auctioneer. That was obvious when she spotted me…because *she did* and when she did, her eyes locked on me like a radar gun-sight…till she made me nervous enough to respond with a nod.

"Sonny" tuned up his guitar with random plunking (it took him a long time), then began to play. Although the musical expertise she had suggested of Sonny was hard to detect, it was better than no music at all. We sang "Rock of Ages," "Bringing in the Sheaves" (that figures) and a few more oldies to get everyone (all thirteen of us) in a religious mood and then she launched into fire and brimstone. She hammered away like Elmer Gantry for an hour or so, then shifted gears into a few more songs and, after the last song…*looked directly at me.*

"Son, come up here and give us a hand," she intoned sugar-sweetly. There was nowhere to run and nowhere to hide. *Trapped!* This old gal really knew how to corner her prey!

Surrendering, I walked to the front. It was time to pass the plate and she had neatly hooked me into serving. The old codger who had arrived early was the other plate-passer. It was hard to believe this was happening. Why did I get into *this?*

The kid twanged away on his strings while the evangelady belted out a song at high volume. The two of us pushed the collection plates at the poor characters sitting there amen-ing and swaying back and forth. Subtracting the geezer and me, there were just four on my side and seven on his. This, in a tent big enough for a hundred or so. Pretty sparse pickings! An estimated total take of about six bucks. Mostly *in change.* Preacher-lady motioned the two of us up to the stage as the kid played. Affecting respectful deference to the best of my ability, I handed my plate to the lady. The other gent did the same.

She peered down into the plates and did a quick mental count.

To my amazement, she charged into another sermon! This one apparently was prepared for just such an occasion. It went on and on about how even Jesus couldn't get by with just a few bucks and, to make it through the Golden Gates, everyone had to open his wallet wide...*and*...we were to *pass the plates again!*

This tiny group of lost souls couldn't possibly have more than a few additional nickels to rub together but, whatever they had, this lady was out to get. Sheepishly, I passed the plate around again on my side as Sonny raised the decibel level of his music to about triple-strength and his mother sang at the top of her lungs. It was the darnedest production I had ever seen, let alone imagined...and I scarcely could believe my being square in the middle of it as a participant.

The good news was that none of the poor folk attending this clambake knew me. Other good news (if it could be called that... from the preacher-lady's point of view) was that after we shoved back the plates, the take was increased by about five more bucks.

At that point, I bailed out and headed for home.

She could be heard moving into her sermon to complete the "saving" of the attending souls. Amazing! She got them to pungle up just about every last dime they had among them. *Elmer Gantry would have been proud!*

Ceremony at start of Vista House construction

Vista House construction was
in process during Word War I.

Columbia Gorge Hotel near Hood River...the early days

Elegant apparel was "de rigueur"
in the Columbia Gorge Hotel.

Meadows along the old highway in the Gorge
Vista House is visible on promontory at top center.

Idea for exciting recreational travel during old highway era.

"Bridge-of-the-Gods" at Cascade Locks

1946 Ford convertible was "hot stuff" during my hitchhiking days.

View east from Vista House

Sign over fireplace in Multnomah Falls Lodge

Classic home on the old highway

Mitchell Point Tunnel on the old highway between Hood River and Mosier. This was blocked after construction of freeway I-84. It has been reconstructed and opened as part of a hiking/biking trail between Hood River and Mosier.

An old truck driver told the story of how on the old highway, his truck and another arrived at opposite ends of a tunnel that had one-way signal lights. The lights were temporarily *malfunctioning.* They each decided to drive through at the same time and met "head-on" in the middle. Because the narrator's truck was a "semi-tractor-trailer" and the other a "truck-trailer" with a more complicated hitch setup, the "semi" had to **back out**. This was routine due to much more difficulty in "backing" a "truck-trailer" rig. He said the problem happened occasionally but caused little difficulty for others on the old highway because it had very light traffic during those early years.

Modern entrance to old Mitchell Point tunnel

The tunnel is located on a closed section of the original historic highway. The Oregon Department Of Transportation has reconstructed the tunnel to make it part of a biking/hiking trail. Although it is part of an outstanding hike or bike ride, the tunnel has been drastically altered for purposes of safety...to the degree that little of its original artistic magic is retained. Most views along this trail are spectacular!

This is the current view near what used to be giant windows (now closed) in old Mitchell Point tunnel.

Sign at east end of Sandy River bridge, Troutdale

We had to earn *our* keep!

Free Spirit at Large

On a few occasions, when my adventuresome spirit won out over schooling, I left home in search of inspiration and excitement. Fortunately, my family would always welcome me back.

In those years, it was reasonably easy for a strong, tall young boy to find various menial temporary jobs…and that is just what I did on my "excursions." Once, hitchhiking in Oregon from Troutdale on the old Columbia River Highway, the night ended in Hood River with no more rides. The entire night was spent sitting (and half-sleeping) under a giant deciduous tree across from a restaurant. All night long, big diesel trucks parked there with engines rumbling as drivers took coffee breaks to relax from the "hairy" runs they had just completed past historic Vista House. No place to sleep wasn't my only problem…it drizzled all night! Didn't get any really deep "sleep."

Next morning, hitching on to The Dalles where the cherry harvest was in full swing, upon arrival I hoofed it down to the railroad station where "rod-riding" hobos typically hung out waiting for farm trucks coming for transient workers. In "them there days," homeless people such as hobos, tramps, bums and hitchhikers had to work for their bread. I loaded in with them bound for a cherry orchard up on nearby hills. At the same time, growing hunger struck! I picked and ate, picked and ate...much more than enough to satisfy my pangs and learned what too much of a good thing can do. For the next three days, the "trots" never left me! So much for "cherry-picking."

Railroad train-hopping "Hobo"

Few knew about it and fewer still will remember... but a quarter mile west of The Dalles railroad station and north over a twenty-foot high rock outcropping, was a place well known to hobos. Beyond that few feet of rock was a partially hidden area surrounded by natural greenery and more rock hummocks. That was the hobo "jungle" where hobos relaxed, cooked and slept. There I shared "Mulligan" stew and slept among the hobos for a few days. What an education!

Bored after a week of cherry picking, hopping a freight train landed me in Pendleton. Low on money again, I quickly learned how good wheat grain can be as food. Pendleton is the grain storage and grain-shipping hub for a vast area of wheat growers. In the train "yards," wheat cars were shuttled to and fro on the tracks and occasionally sprung small "leaks." The result was little piles of wheat accumulated along the tracks. Just scoop up

Rides in trucks on the old road could be "hairy" propositions ...when passing with only inches to spare.

a handful and start chewing. That's when one learns wheat grains turn "gummy" when chewed.

Then I hit the jackpot for more free food. A hobo exclaimed, "Hey, check that reefer (refrigerator car) over there...it's got a whole bunch of produce." Yeah...it had "produce" all right! It was an old refrigerator car that had ice compartments in each end. The shipping company (United Fruit) had three-hundred pound blocks of ice placed in each end of the car at the start of the trip...and more ice blocks were added at stops along the way to keep the shipments cool and fresh. The railroad had ice-making plants strategically located throughout the nation for this purpose.

The car the hobo referred me to had been full of watermelons shipped from California. Standing on tiptoes and peeking into the car, the sight was amazing. A couple of feet of straw covered the floor on which the load had been bedded softly...and there were still a hundred or so melons in the car. I hopped up into the car to feast on the free goodies...and was chagrined to find them all rotten. That was when I learned the lesson that a half-rotten watermelon still has an edible heart. Melons rot from the outside in and the hearts rot last. Although on the squishy side (beggars can't be choosers), that amounted to a much appreciated psuedo-meal.

After telling the same hobo that I had no place to stay...he suggested we go to the "Sally" and get a "duckit". Yep. Hobo terms for the Salvation Army! According to him, they would give anybody in need a ticket for a meal and a cot for one night's lodging. Destitute and in no mood to spend the night outside, I went along with him to the Sally.

Unknowing, it shocked me to discover people who offered help to those in need with a "no questions asked" policy. We slept the night there and both got a free dinner to boot.

That stay became one of the most expensive of my life! Since then, although I've stayed in numerous top hotels around the world, that brief interlude cost me more. So impressed was I with the Salvation Army's selfless attitude and help- fulness in lifting a restive kid out of temporary difficulty that, in years

Hobo's smoke of choice ..."roll your own" for...*five cents!*

that followed, I gave and gave and gave to them. Dang! I'm still giving them money and items. Once, highly insulted by a car dealership offering me peanuts to trade in a late model vehicle on a new one...I told them to forget it, drove it to the nearest Salvation Army unit and signed the title over to them. They drove it happily for the next ten years. Another time, a fine conference table, plus ten matching upholstered chairs, became surplus. When it required too much "monkey-motion" to sell them, I loaded them up and delivered them to the "Sally."

Maybe they should take in more "runaway" kids!

It can be windy in the Gorge...limbs are blown to west side of Douglas fir trees at Chanticleer Point...and to east side of trees upriver.

I hitchhiked rides in diesel trucks like this on the old highway.

45

Douglas fir forests blanket steep mountains in the Gorge.

The old highway had many tight curves...and a number
of giant trees were surprisingly close to the edges.

Psychology 101

The fact that one of my file folders held forty-two assorted traffic tickets when the Army drafted me isn't the issue. Hey…couldn't anybody have ordinary bad luck and get quite a lot of traffic citations? It was simply that I drove a lot more than most and, yes, considerably faster, made more noise and maybe added a few more wild driving antics than others and, well, yeah...*a lot more!*

The Army made me a changed man. There is nothing like going from earning big money to making itsy-bitsy draftee pay to get a guy's attention. There were a lot of other things in the military that got my attention: like being Army-school trained as a clerk-typist and arriving in "downtown" Germany to find my new outfit didn't need clerks but did need the lowliest of all…"mechanics' helpers."

Yep. That's me. *A mechanic's helper!*

At least, that's how my tour started. The fact that it ended with me rated Specialist Fourth Class...with two Sergeants First Class, two "buck" Sergeants, two Corporals, two twelve-man squads, two 2 ½ ton trucks and two 3/4 tons, two Jeeps, six drivers and two interpreters all reporting directly to me...*is another story.* But, that *is* how it ended. Hard to believe? Nope! That's just *how the army operates.*

At any rate, my stint in the Army really calmed me down and helped tame some of my wilder tendencies. By the time my honorable discharge was handed me, I was ready to be John Q. Goodcitizen. *No more wild stuff!*

After my release from the army, I became a construction contractor. As a result, it worked out that visits to the Pacific coast and the interior of Oregon were necessary. So much mileage was put on my truck that worry about having breakdowns became a consideration. The answer was to buy a brand-new pickup truck.

Two days after acquiring the truck, my schedule was set to drive up the Columbia Gorge to a project in the state's interior. Eighteen-year-old "Bart" was working for me during the summer helping me on work contracted for beyond the Cascade mountain range. Bart arrived ready for work early the morning of our planned trip east. The pickup was pulling a large trailer loaded with supplies and equipment but *there was a problem.*

The new truck had been ordered with large extended rear-view side mirrors but they did not arrive with the truck. This is not considered much of a problem for most small truck owners but most do not use a truck the way we did. My truck and trailer were usually loaded to the maximum with equipment and supplies...to the point of almost hanging overboard. Large wide mirrors are an absolute requirement to see adequately to the rear past the trailer and, on this day, *they were not yet on the truck.*

As we drove toward the old Columbia River Highway, we talked about the mirror problem and decided to stop at a small town to buy the correct mirrors. Arriving at a dealership, the parts people were asked if they had the big mirrors. Nope. Didn't have them. Well...didn't really think they would...we were hoping against hope. Stopping had been a waste of time.

We drove on, deciding to be extra cautious and not pull out in front of other vehicles without doing a careful "look-see" before acting.

Bart was unusual for an eighteen-year-old...much more responsible and under control than others his age. Must have been his upbringing. He was bright and could talk intelligently on a number of subjects. Also, he understood clearly that his job was to help me make a profit. These attributes make such a kid a delight to have around and we had a lot of fun working together.

Near Bridal Veil, we drove over a rise in the road...and smack ahead appeared a state policeman located in a strategic position for nailing anyone who might be breaking a law. *I cringed.*

Sure enough, as we passed by he waved me over.

He walked up to the truck window, looked in and said, "Good

morning, Sir. You have 'obstructed rear vision.'" He stated it emphatically...but very politely.

"Well, ah...er...ah...yes, guess so," I replied...kicking myself mentally for not addressing my lack of proper mirrors well before starting the trip.

The policeman was young, handsome, clean cut and as nice as can be—much nicer and pleasant than most of the pushy cops who had given me so many tickets only a few years earlier.

"You know, Sir, that 'obstructed rear vision' can create dangerous driving conditions for others on the road?"

"Yes, that's true," I sheepishly replied, "And you're certainly correct for pointing it out. The fact is, we stopped earlier and tried to buy the correct mirrors for the truck but they didn't have them in stock...and we have a job to do over the mountain...so we......."

It was quite obvious that the law had simply been disregarded and we had continued our trip lacking the proper equipment.

"Well Sir, it is a clear violation and it does pose a real danger on the highway so I feel obligated to cite you for it."

It was apparent that he was a gentleman the way he was going about his explanation. For the first time in my life, I was getting a traffic ticket and feeling OK about accepting it. That didn't mean I was happy about it...not even a little bit...but this time, I'd take my medicine without "whining." The thought almost shocked me! He wrote the citation and handed it to me...with courtesy and a pleasant demeanor.

As he walked away, Bart called out to him. "Sir, I see you have a 'radar gun' in your car. Would you mind showing me how it works?"

That caught both the policeman and me by surprise. This kid had a lot more going for him than I had realized. He truly was interested in the radar gun and not a bit reticent about asking the policeman to show and explain it to him...even under our somewhat adverse circumstances.

Radar guns were a relatively new speed enforcement tool and were definitely a mystery to most motorists. Everybody hated them and few knew much about them.

The lawman graciously invited Bart over to the car and proceeded to give him a lesson on the application of radar. Watching from my truck, Bart seemed to be engaging him in what appeared to be intelligent

Chanticleer Point "readerboard"

Board text describing origin of the great highway:

"Sam Hill, an eccentric and wealthy railroad attorney, was a passionate "good roads" enthusiast with a flair for publicity. On August 27, 1913, Hill and other advocates for a Columbia River Highway, met with Multnomah County Commissioners on this bluff at the Chanticleer Inn. With this dramatic vista in the background, Hill and engineer Samuel C. Lancaster outlined the vision of a scenic highway where "tired men and women... may enjoy the wild beauty of nature's art gallery and recreate themselves." Construction surveys were under way within a month and by the 1920s the Historic Columbia River Highway was called the 'King of Roads.'"

"Chanticleer Inn, constructed in 1912, occupied this bluff until destroyed by fire in 1931. The inn was one of several roadhouses providing elegant accommodations for travelers along the Historic Columbia River Highway at the dawn of the automobile age."

conversation so I got out, walked over and joined them.

The young officer was quite thoughtful and explained it all again for me. We watched for a while as he aimed the "gun" at passing vehicles and let us read the results on its display. All in all, his stopping us had turned into a somewhat fun experience learning about radar (the citation received notwithstanding). We spent a good thirty minutes observing and making small talk, then turned to bid him goodbye.

As we walked away, he called out to me. "Sir, would you please come back for a moment?"

What had I done now? The traffic ticket should be enough.

He held out his hand. "Would you please give me the citation I just issued you."

My first thought was, "Man alive, what the heck is this going to be?"

"Why do you want it?"

He replied, "Upon thinking about it, I've decided you already have learned your lesson and you've convinced me you will do something to correct it at your first opportunity."

Well…he was darn sure right about that.

"Please give the citation back to me!"

Even after many years have passed from the time of this incident, it is still hard to believe my next utterance.

"No…*I'm not going to give it back.*"

Policeman: "*Just hand it back to me.*"

Me: "No, you were right. You did the best job of any policeman I've ever dealt with in explaining it. You were courteous. It would not be a good lesson for my young friend here if I were to give it back. *I will keep it.*"

Policeman: "Ok, Ok…that's all fine and good. *Just hand me the citation, please.*"

Me: "*No!*"

This continued to astound both of them and…*me.*

We were all shocked. This was the most unlikely interchange imaginable.

But…*I meant it.* I had it coming and, for the first time in my life, was willing to suffer the consequences of my infraction. And it *really was* the truth as to my feelings about the impression this would make on Bart.

Commemorative bronzes at Chanticleer Point

Native American bronze detail...a village beside the river

Bart was way beyond speechless. He knew me to be a bit of a harmless "con-man." Not a predatory type…(simply as a good salesman). That is necessary to be successful in any business. He had watched me in action bending some people to my point of view. My term for it is "negotiating." He wasn't sure now, though, just what was going on. Was this guy getting "conned"…*or what??*

Policeman to me: "Well…tell you what. The whole idea is for you to become a better driver and I think that will happen so (as he opened his citation book to the original copies) I'm just going to tear all of these out….*RRRIIIIPPPPP*….and you are going to look a little foolish when you go into court and appear for a citation that doesn't exist." He then proceeded to tear the paper into smaller bits and stuff them in his pocket.

"Gotta get back to work," he said, oh, so nicely…then turned and walked back to his car, got in and drove away.

We stood for a moment absolutely stunned. Had this really happened? Were we dreaming? Had I just fought over the keeping of a nasty "Moving Violation" citation and…lost? Or…won?

Bart wondered, "Wow, did Marc con this guy or what?"

You can believe we talked about it almost incessantly for the rest of the drive and frequently the next few days. Bart would tell the story to anyone who would listen. He thought it was one of the neatest things he had ever witnessed. It was continually necessary to defend my position with him and remind him that, yes, I had been perfectly willing to accept that ticket. He had a hard time believing it. To him, it looked a lot like an exceedingly slick con-job…well, *sort of*. However, it really *wasn't* a con-job. At the moment of receiving the ticket, it was my intention to see it through.

During this period, my hobby had been learning about antique automobiles and airplanes. In two or three years of intense involvement and observation, enough was learned about the famed Model T Ford that some considered me an expert on the subject. Buying and selling old car parts, mostly for the sport of it, I soon came to know almost all the variations of every "T" part manufactured by Ford over the full nineteen-year production run of the Model T. Henry produced over fifteen million of them and made a heck of a lot of changes during that period and…I knew most of them.

Three weeks after the bizarre event with the policeman, a local Ford Model T Club asked me to be guest speaker at their next general meet-

Old cars were a lot of fun...author's 1910 Franklin

Aerobatic antique airplane proved to be exciting sport
(Meyers "OTW" with Kinner 5-cylinder engine)

Before attempting "aerobatics," It seemed a good idea to do a bit of parachute jumping "just to get the feel"...*in the event of dire necessity!* At the time, readily available war-surplus parachute canopies used for the purpose were too small for my weight...and a few practice jumps resulted in extremely hard landings with a couple of nasty sprains and contusions.

Corbett Country Market
on the old highway

Concrete bridges on the old Columbia River
Highway were a wonder of their day.

ing. They said the talk could be on any related subject of my choosing. Agreeing to address their group, "*Psychology*" was my choice.

While searching for old car parts over the period of a few years, a number of important lessons had been learned in the psychology of getting people to part with old belongings. Aging owners of remnants from antique autos could be quirky about whether they would part with pieces of the past. Maybe they remembered good times in that rusty old pile in the back forty or had some other significant memory attached to it that made it hard for them to let it go.

Studying the art of making friends with such people, I had learned how to broach the subject of acquiring parts from them at precisely the right time. Didn't always work but my record was fairly good...and it was all due to applying primary psychology.

To augment my talk, I put six different types of hats in a cardboard box...and headed for the meeting. My plan was to illustrate how different approaches can be used in dealing with people by changing hats and, in effect, playing completely different roles...much as an actor. Many of the folks in farming communities were suspicious of anyone seeming to be a slick "flat-land foreigner" and better rapport was achieved by appearing to be "one of their kind." These measures were necessary to realize higher degrees of success...and *they were proven.*

At the meeting, the president of the group ushered me and my box of hats to the front and introduced me as the first item on the agenda...the "*guest speaker.*" Taking my position on the podium, I glanced out over the crowd...then along the front row.

No! Impossible! It couldn't be! It WAS!

The same courteous and friendly policeman (*the very policeman who had torn up my citation*) was sitting in the *front row! He* was a *member* of the Model T Club.

This was my best presentation for the purpose and the entire content was about how to...well...not exactly "*con*" but "*how to persuade*" people to one's point of view in sensitive circumstances. Most people do what might be considered "conning" in attempts to get others to do ordinary things such as buying a car, renewing insurance or getting kids to eat their cereal.

Going through the entire presentation, I changed all six hats and my appearance and basic personality with each. Having prepared only the one talk to give, my thought was "Hope the policeman has a sense of humor."

He *did not* exhibit a sense of humor. *He was not amused!* He wouldn't look at me or talk to me after the meeting. Obviously, he assumed he had been hoodwinked out on the highway...*but it just wasn't so.*

That bothered me for years.

He had been considerably more polite and explanatory than typical policemen...and I truly did appreciate his gentlemanly attitude when he made clear why he thought it necessary to cite me.

It really *was not* a con-job on the highway!

Bart still isn't sure.

Author on unicycle he rode up Multnomah Falls trail **at night** ... ...after a few salutary "libations!"

Dragon sculpture aside highway west of Springdale

The "Wild west" is alive and well at Springdale on the old highway.

Hunting geese and pheasants along Columbia River
could be one heck of a lot of fun.

Just The Bare Facts

There aren't a lot of people who can say they have rowed a "rubber" (inflatable) boat across the wide Columbia River. But a friend of mine and I can honestly make that claim. And we did it with Vista House lights in sight...*at night!* The word "rubber" is appropriate because our boat was a well-used WWII "surplus" emergency life raft...and that was the term used at the time by stores selling war leftovers.

A late fall evening was approaching as we rounded a turn on the old highway below grand old Vista House. Arriving up at the front of the building, we circled it to park facing the river. Bill reached down and scooped up his binoculars. We both jumped out and walked over to the low rock wall to gaze down on the massive Columbia. We stood there transfixed by what surely is one of the most striking river viewpoints in the entire United States.

Bill raised his "glasses" and adjusted the focus. Then he began to scan the river and its surroundings...seven-hundred thirty feet below.

It was goose-hunting season and we had just come from far upriver where our hunting expedition had begun at three A.M. It was a long day and we were on our way home when Bill suggested we stop at Vista House and, from its superb viewpoint, check the river below for geese that might have found their way there. Our luck had been nil upriver and we thought there might be one more skinny possibility of bagging a bird down along the river's shores.

For a few minutes, Bill scanned back and forth looking upriver and down. Just as he was about to give up, he let our a little yelp. "Oh boy…there's a small flock of geese flying west and looking for a place to spend the night. They'll most likely land on the island just west of Lower Corbett. Let's hop in the truck and head down the hill."

Bill proposed the idea of inflating our boat and using it to chase across the river after the birds. We had carried it with us on this day of hopeful goose hunting and had planned to use it upriver but had no reason to remove it from its protective case.

Arriving at Lower Corbett, we shot across the new overpass and onto the slick new stretch of road in the direction of Portland. Traffic was light…only a lone vehicle now and then…a far cry from what it would be only a few years hence.

We quickly drove a half-mile along the highway and parked on the shoulder directly across from a small island. Bill was right! He hopped out excitely and trained his glasses on the island. "Yup… *there they are!*", he exclaimed. "*Let's pump the boat.*"

Speedily, we jerked the boat out of the truck bed and out of its case, assembled the pump, hooked it up and Bill pumped like mad to fill the boat with air. Meanwhile, I tossed the oars together and raced with them and our guns down the steep rocky bank to the river's edge.

Returning uphill, I joined Bill in hiking the fully inflated boat down to the water. We threw our guns into the boat and piled in. With darkness now only minutes away, I began rowing like a wild man! The slower autumn current made it much easier to cross the river than at any other time of year. However…we made one big mistake–a classic of less-experienced boatmen. We had entered the water directly across the river from where the geese had settled. Even with the slower-than-usual current, it was so far across the river (almost a mile) that, by the time we reached the island, the current had taken us more than a half-mile downriver from the location of the geese.

The good news? Our location would allow us to stalk the birds by moving inland through trees where they couldn't see us. The bad news? We were now a long way from them and it was dusk...with darkness rapidly approaching.

Arriving on the island's shore, we pulled the boat up high, grabbed the guns and sprinted up the beach. The geese were right at the shoreline. Not to "spook" them, we moved into dense trees about three hundred yards from them and walked gingerly upriver until we figured we were even with the geese. We couldn't see them through the trees so it was just a guess where they were.

Easing silently through the trees, we got a peek ...and *there they were* in front of us approximately two hundred yards distant. Bill flipped a coin and, in a whisper, asked me to "Call it." Tails turned up so it was up to me to run out to the birds.

As quietly as possible, I slipped a shell into the chamber of my gun...jumped up...and began a run directly at the birds. Ten steps hadn't been covered when the geese spotted me, hopped into the water and began paddling away from shore. We assumed the geese then would fly. *Nope!* They just paddled straight out away from shore. By the time I reached the water's edge, the birds had paddled out about forty yards. *Then* they spread their wings and began a takeoff...at the same time I moved my shotgun up in one fast sweeping motion and fired.

It appeared that one had been hit...but not for certain because it dropped back to the water and resumed paddling. For some reason, it didn't fly.

Taking decisive action, I placed the gun on the sand, took off my high-topped boots, rolled my trousers up to my knees, picked up my gun and plunged into the wintry cold water.

Wading toward the paddling goose while avoiding underwater holes made progress slow. For reasons known only to the goose, it was paddling slowly but, like the brilliant strategists they are, it stayed just a shade beyond the reach of the gun's effectiveness. Its slow movement reinforced my thinking that it must have been "winged" and that made my resolve to get to him ironclad. Even with the shallow water and my pants rolled up, it was obvious *more drastic measures were necessary!*

Rushing back to shore and laying down my gun, I whipped my

Our goose "quarries" sailed right over this sign location
on their way to the island of our folly.

Our "goose adventure" island...from Vista House

pants and shorts off! Bill couldn't believe his eyes...but this was no time for discussion! Grabbing my gun and wheeling around, I plunged back into the water and swiftly waded to regain lost advantage. All the while, the goose had been paddling slowly away. By the time I'd covered two hundred yards from shore, the river was up to my shirt tail and the goose still wasn't close enough...and man, oh man, *that water was cold!*

Then a second wild decision! The goose's progress had slowed and it still seemed to be within the gun's range...if the water gap could be closed enough...so, back to shore once again.

Bill was there to greet me...cracked-up with laughter. In no mood to joke, I hadn't yelled "uncle" yet. Stripping off the rest of my clothes, I charged back into the river with my gun over my head and waded like crazy! *Too late!* By the time armpit depth was reached, the bird had paddled out too far and it was now too dark to see.

Wading back to shore with chattering teeth, I found Bill still howling over the entire "scene." Because of the icy cold, my mood was not nearly as light as his!

We decided to run back to the boat figuring that, by running, my body temperature would increase. So...with me *buck-naked*...we ran! At the boat, Bill took off his jacket, handed it to me and began rowing as fast as he could all the way back across the river in pitch-blackness. Again, we lost headway and drifted even further downstream.

Arriving on shore with my teeth still chattering non-stop, we left the boat behind to be picked up later and hoofed it back up to the highway and our truck. There was no point in putting on wet pants or shorts...so the entire distance was covered with me naked from the waist down.

We were surprised when I did not get pneumonia from this dizzy event.

Maybe you're wondering, "Are there hunters who are that crazy about hunting...and who *would really do something like that?*"

Yep. *There are...*and *we did!*

Sandy River bridge at Troutdale...
Entrance to many of my adventures on the Historic Columbia River Highway
Airplane visible in upper right is on final approach to Troutdale Airport
...where I earned my pilot's license in later years.

Transoceanic

Have you ever wanted something so badly that it became your secret obsession?

The cost was way over my head but the dream of having it just kept gnawing away on my subconscious. When the thought of possession crept into my thinking, I would visualize it enhancing my activities.

My interest had been aroused after seeing it advertised in a National Geographic Magazine...that good old magazine with all the ads for exotic world cruises. Those flashy ads were fantasy to my young brain... the very idea of having enough money beyond groceries and gas was unimaginable! Who *were* these people who would be moved to action by such ads? And *where* did they get that kind of money? My resources were only enough to allow riding in a rowboat! Nevertheless, my heart's desire was *also* advertised there. It was mixed in between the assorted ads for train trips beyond my means, fancy cotton-rag stationery way over my head, exotic movie cameras that were only a dream and a whole lot of other stuff that only could be fantasized. Although all of that was unaffordable for me...surely the day would come when it would be possible to have that one outstanding possession...*and I began to save money for it.*

I don't remember how we met...but it's easy to remember clearly how sweet and pixie-like pretty she was. And "charmed" wasn't the word...I was *captivated!* Another "prospect" had entered my life!

This little gal had it all. A perfect body, perfect poise, perfect voice, perfect...it went on and on. And guess what? She *liked me!* I began to visualize a future with her. You've done that, haven't you? You know what I mean. In your mind's eye you've seen the two of you waltzing through life together forever and ever, amen! A lifetime of excitement, joy, happiness, children...and then old age in rockers side by side...*that kind of thing*. You've done that. You can't kid me! That's how far gone *I was* on her. As usual, it was important to execute some unique escapades to impress her.

At 16, I worked in "the woods" (timber and lumber industry) and had learned a fair amount about logging equipment and how to run some of it. I planned to demonstrate my talents to this gal by finding a large machine to operate *right before her eyes!*

We drove far into the Cascade mountain range where the giant timber was virgin...and arrived at an active logging "show."

Hold everything!...a bit of explanation is required here:

A logging "show" is a large area of timber in the process of being felled and bucked...then to be trucked to a sawmill. "Falling" is cutting the trees down and "bucking" is cutting the logs to shorter lengths.

At the time, logging shows on steep mountain terrain had a tall "topped" Douglas fir "spar" tree stripped of limbs and "rigged" with cable "stays" from the remaining "stub" top to hold it in place. The stay cables fanned out in all directions from the spar and were anchored to large stumps. The spar-tree was further rigged with large "blocks" ("sheaves" or "pulleys" to the non-mechanical) through which cables passed from a giant "triple-drum" power-winch machine ("yarder") positioned alongside. A "main" cable ran from the yarder up the tree to a block on top, then down the hill to "chokers" connected to bucked logs. The logs were "yarded" (pulled) up the hill to the "landing" (flat spot for piling and loading logs onto trucks). The complete setup was called a "High-lead Show." I hope you got that...because there might be a quiz later!

In addition to the spar tree and triple-drum winch-yarder arrangement, there would be a *giant caterpillar-type tractor* nearby for purposes of road building and heavy pushing/pulling duties.

That was my target!

Good news. Not a soul in sight! The place was completely abandoned for the weekend.

We stretched in glorious sunshine and scouted the area. The little gal definitely was impressed with the monumental size of everything. Logging shows in virgin timber are a bit overwhelming…*everything* is on a gigantic scale!

Hand in hand, we sauntered over to the caterpillar tractor (about eight times bigger than my pickup and about the size of her house). I hoisted her up about six feet onto the top of the Cat's steel track. We then climbed together to the operator's seat. The machine was an "International TD-24," the biggest "Cat" in the world at the time. It was magnificent!

No ignition key was required…so…*I fired it up!*

Then…with the pretty little sprite sitting at my side, I displayed my equipment-operating prowess by shoving piles of dirt bigger than my truck, extending a new logging road and pushing over a couple of twenty-four-inch trees. The power of this giant machine was astounding. Although my actions were a "bit" illegal, care was taken not to do any damage…just push a few things around which the regular Cat operator would be doing later as part of his job.

A little "aside": Amazingly, about thirty years later, it was my pleasure to be a guest at occasional parties given by the same family who owned the giant timber company operating this big "Cat." Will wonders never cease…and *may they never read this book!*

Finally, enough money was accumulated to buy the "dream" item described earlier. It was slightly used but, nonetheless, an absolute beauty. *I was ecstatic!* This was going to be my tool to unlock the heart and soul of my cute little gal. Five minutes after picking it up, I called her for a picnic date.

We left on a Saturday morning. Destination…right up the famous historic old Columbia River Highway with its romantic beauty of natural surroundings.

We stopped first at grand old Vista House on Crown Point…and took in the striking view. Then, it was over the mountains into gloriously warm and beautiful forests on the edge of the high desert country.

My plan for the day had been worked out carefully and all the right equipment was packed: a brand new cooler full of beer and pop, plenty of potato chip crunchies and sandwiches, fruit, some veggies, a big soft blanket and…*my new secret weapon… my dream realized…my ZENITH TRANSOCEANIC SHORT-WAVE RADIO!!!* Yep…you got it! *All twenty pounds of it.*

Upper Alex Barr Road past Vista House was a great place for dating kids to park and spark.

Basking in the sun at Vista House

That was the goody so supremely expensive and hard to come by …*now right in my hot hands.* The batteries alone cost more than most ordinary portable radios. This absolutely was going to guarantee success in the achievement of ardent romance.

The radio was advertised as able to bring in stations from the Orient, Europe, Africa, Australia, Russia, Mongolia, Cucamonga, Podunk and Timbuktu. This baby, *according to the ads,* could do it all! Finally, it could bring romantic music into distant boondocks…a concept made in heaven…and a necessity for any guy wishing to woo with pizzazz.

A super-special spot for the day's action was pre-selected and down pat. It was an abandoned Forest Service lookout station in a high wooden tower on an Indian reservation. Scoped out a couple of months earlier, it was calculated to be just about as romantic as a gondola in Venice…without the snoopy oarsman looking over impassioned shoulders.

We arrived at ground-zero beneath the soaring tower about eleven o'clock in the morning. The day was cloudless…temperature about eighty degrees…humidity around thirty-five…latitude near forty-five…longitude not exactly certain…pulse (mine)…about two-hundred and ready to rock and roll. Hoped she was, too…if you catch the drift. You don't? *You haven't been paying attention!*

We shifted drinks to a hand-carry cooler, put all the food and crunchies in a pack and grabbed the giant (no…*behemoth*) Zenith Transoceanic. Then we trudged straight up about a hundred and fifty wooden stairs. Before we could, however, we had to first break though a permanent barrier. Didn't remember seeing the "*Danger, Condemned*" sign before! Figured that must be new. It gave me pause but, what the heck, we were here and there wasn't a soul in sight. So, *up we went.*

It was a spooky ascent because the wood steps creaked and shook and the whole tower swayed back and forth in an increasing warm morning breeze. The climb was about ten times more nerve-wracking than might have been imagined. This tower *really was* ready to collapse. We were halfway up before we realized how shaky it was. Near the bottom sections it was still fairly stable being fastened to the ground but up high…man, oh man, it swayed and shook.

If I was a little nervous, my poor gal friend needed heavy-duty reassurances that we were going to live through this whole experience…

not exactly conducive to relaxed "sparking." So, after making it to the top, rolling out the blanket and then settling down to a nice lunch, I set about rigging up my secret weapon...and extracted the neat telescoping antenna.

As any romantic knows, a situation like this demands the finest of soft music to put the finishing touches on such a well-thought-out plan.

Ceremoniously, I punched the "ON" button.

Hmmm......*static!*

Well...there were a lot more buttons to go. This jewel had over a dozen where most radios had only two or three to press.

Another button.

More *static!*

A third and a fourth.

Static, static!

A fifth and sixth!

Static, static, static!

I dialed, twisted, pushed and tapped on it...then punched every last one of those damn cute little buttons with tiny print next to them indicating this instrument could get reception from countries all over the entire known world.

Static, static, static, static!

Why the heck couldn't it get at least one decent music station somewhere? This monster had cost a ton of money!

Finally, after ten minutes of messing around with it, I gave up and zeroed in on a local broadcast station that was reasonably clear.

Country music!

My god!

She hated country music.

The rest of the story is rather anti-climactic. Romance without music is like *fishing without bait.* Well...that's about it. That doggone fancy radio never did perform remotely close to what the glowing advertisements promised...and I've never wholly believed another advertisement to this very day.

Zenith *"Transoceanic"*

This is the hotshot monster radio that was supposed to be a fantastic performer and pull stations in from thousands of miles away. When I needed it most, all I could squeeze out of it was a lot of static and a less than stellar local station. It weighed in at around twenty pounds......and *cost a bundle.*

Crown Point and Vista House high above Interstate highway I-84.

Indians "dip-netting" salmon at Celilo before dam construction
One of the most striking river views in America...
...now *just a memory!*

Mosier Valley Post Office

Columbia River, from Cascade Locks to The Dalles,
is wind-surfers paradise...note "boards" on top of vehicle.

"Twin Tunnels" hiking/biking trail between Hood River and Mosier
(a closed section of the old highway)

Freight trains are a lot snazzier these days...and when
did you last see a real "hobo" on one of them?

(photo taken from Multnomah Falls parking lot)

Steam engines were powerful...and *fast!*

Jackhammered

As hard as it might be for a modern kid to believe, getting a ride "hitchhiking" on highways used to be amazingly easy and fruitful. The old Columbia River Highway saw more than its fair share of hitchhikers...partly because it was so astoundingly scenic. Hitchhiking was an accepted way of travel. That all changed with the "Hippie" era of the nineteen-sixties when kids grew long hair, whiskers and beards, wore crazy clothing and, in general, began to look sloppy, dirty and fruit-loopy and some...downright scary.

Before that time, hitchhikers were from many walks of life. One could see college kids trying to save a buck "hitching" to and from school, itinerant workers heading for an agricultural harvest somewhere, kids skipping school and going nowhere in general and, sometimes, a kid like me leaving home after deciding he wasn't suitably "understood" or just searching for adventure. It was my nature to "take off" if things around home got a little dicey for me, particularly because I found school attendance boring and skipped regularly. The school's "one-size-fits-all" curriculum didn't match my aptitudes.

A type of person one would *never* see "thumbing" a ride was a "hobo." "Hobos" were men (and *very rarely* "hoboettes") who rode "freight" trains. Completely different breeds of cat, they stuck together as much as total strangers doing the same things can stick together. I can't remember ever seeing a hobo hitchhiking. However, a lot of hitchhikers rode freight trains. It just didn't seem to work the other way around. Possibly a main reason for that was the hobo's typical dress. They were inclined to be a scruffy bunch because the trains they rode were "steam" powered and spewed out large clouds of soot that found its way onto their clothes. There was little or no access to true cleanliness in hobo "jungles," usually woodsy areas near railroad tracks. Many of the "homeless" people on the streets today likely would have been hobos in days of old.

Seldom seen on a highway was anyone appearing dirty or messy. Hitchhikers then were a much cleaner and neater group. It was tough to get a ride if one didn't appear reasonably clean but…if one did (and most hitchhikers did), a ride would usually materialize in a fairly short time. I remember getting a ride (at age sixteen) from Minnesota all the way to central Idaho with a proper young man and wife. We had a wonderful time gabbing and enjoying the scenery. Try that today. Never happen! Those types of people whiz right on by anyone on the road even remotely resembling someone wanting a ride. The general assumption these days is that the guy "thumbing" for a ride might have left the scene of a triple axe murder minutes ago…and was one of the participants…and today they frequently look the part!

The reasons people picked hitchhikers up ran the gamut. Nice people would pick up a clean-appearing person simply to do a "good deed." Many lone drivers simply wanted company. Perhaps ten-percent of truck drivers would pick up hitchhikers. Most of the biggest trucks had "No Rider" signs clearly posted on their windshields. That didn't necessarily mean a truck driver wouldn't pick up a guy with his thumb out. It just meant that was company policy. As a hitchhiker, I rode many times behind a "No Rider" sign in a large truck. These fellows got lonely and bored on runs such as steep mountain grades…back when trucks were so underpowered they ground away up hills at low speed…creating long lines of frustrated drivers behind them.

A hitchhiker getting a ride in a truck on the old Columbia River Highway could expect a hair-raising experience. The rider would be exposed to stretches so narrow that mirrors on the right side of the truck would almost touch giant rock cliffs and humongous Douglas fir trees. That's how close a truck had to operate near obstructions on the narrow roads. As a rider, it scared the living daylights out of me to see massive cliffs approaching on my side like apparitions out of a horror movie. There were places where trucks passed each other with only inches to spare. In a truck, the old highway was one electrifying trip!

It wasn't all roses for all hitchhikers. A friend watched a car rush past in a heavy snowstorm… to crash only minutes later into another vehicle a few miles ahead. The speedy car had rolled a couple of times and discharged a hitchhiking passenger. Sadly, the hitchhiker was dead. The errant driver was drunk. A caveat of hitchhiking: the hitcher cannot guess the competency of a driver until *after* getting into the car…and, for that reason, hitchhiking can be a "chancy" proposition. However, people then didn't seem to be in such crazy hurries as they are today. I recall getting rides with farmers, the owner of a large auto dealership, an RKO Radio Pictures "generator" truck, a man going to a new job in a mountain lodge, a school teacher and a couple of aggressive homosexuals who tried to put the make on me. In general, drivers were surprisingly friendly and helpful. What the heck has made all of that go away?

One late afternoon found me (at age 13) "thumbing" on the old Columbia Highway when a fish company's "refrigerated" truck stopped. The driver was headed to Pendleton…and that was fine with me.

By the time we got to the old "Rowena Loops," it was dark. We wound our way down through the switchbacks and drove through The Dalles. We saw tugboats and barges in the tiny canal that ran eight miles beside the highway giving them the ability to get past Celilo Falls. That was back when the falls still existed and boat traffic had to circumvent them…before The Dalles dam created a lake that made the falls disappear…and took away one of America's most awe-inspiring natural sights.

Before the dam was constructed, Indians, having "sovereign" fishing rights, dipped nets for giant salmon on unbelievably dangerous spindly jury-rigged platforms over wildly raging waters. Just watching them was scary. That was one more case of many beautiful wild rivers and historic sights eliminated by modern dams.

Added to the old highway's slow pace were the fish delivery stops. We arrived in Pendleton about four in the morning and I was able to hoof it three miles to the nearest hobo "jungle" in the still dark cool air. In late August, Pendleton gets hotter than Hades with daytime temperatures often reaching over 100°.

Hobos always knew where to get temporary work and that was my goal. A job turned up the first day working on a wheat ranch tossing "hay-swath" bundles up onto a WWII surplus "six-by-six" army truck. The "jungle" stay lasted eight days. It was near the railroad yards so, when I decided to return home, it was a simple matter of hopping another freight train. Unfortunately, the ride turned out to be anything but simple.

The train selected was truly unusual. It had only one "open" car in the middle of the entire three-quarter mile string of cars...which would have been fine...had it been a "box-car." *It wasn't!* It was a "gondola" filled with a double-high stack of heavy railroad car wheels attached to axles. All of the boxcars on the train were full, locked and sealed.

A "gondola" is a car with sides about half as high as a typical "box-car" and wide open at the top. The fact that the gondola was chockfull of the wheel-axles did not appear at first to present a problem. It seemed a matter of simply sitting *under* the load and riding it out. Hopping in and making myself at home beneath the mammoth wheel-axles combinations proved no problem. They were loaded tightly...so there was no worry about one moving and whacking off an arm or a leg.

The train rolled slowly out from the railroad "yards" and moved onto the "main line" to Portland. So far...so good!

When the train began to pick up serious speed, my comfortable situation under the big axles began to take on an entirely different flavor. A distinctive sharp "*clack*" began to sound. As the train gained even more speed, the "clack" increased in tempo right along with the speed. At first, it was just a unique sound...but, as the speed quickened, an exceedingly sharp impact arrived with each "clack."

Now on the "main line," the train moved to an even higher speed! It had one of the last giant steam-locomotives pulling it...and man, *this baby could move!*

The train maxxed out at around seventy miles an hour and the little "clack" had now transitioned to a wicked snapping jolt. Furthermore, it was clacking and sharply jolting with every turn of the train's wheels. In the relatively few times I had ridden freights, no hobo had ever told me about the infamous "*flat wheel*" car. Alas! *Trapped like a rat*—in the only rideable car on the train...with a villainous matched pair of *flat wheel*s.

The evil "flat wheel" is caused by one axle locking up when a train's brakes are applied…thereby dragging the "fixed" wheel-axle combination until both wheels are ground flat at one point…causing the car to bounce sharply with each wheel revolution.

The jolts now arrived so close together and so hard that sitting down would have damaged my body beyond repair. The jolts actually jerked the car up and down as fast as a machine-gun. Holy mackerel! "*Trainzilla*" was killing me!

Kneeling to absorb and minimize the incessant hammering proved ineffective. That could be maintained for only less than a minute. The constant *whack-whack-whack-whack* producing violent shocks at high speed was taking a toll on my body…but the train kept right on hammering with no letup.

The beating became so bad that it was necessary to work my way under the axles to the car's end and climb to the top railing, then reach across to the ladder fixed on the end of the adjoining boxcar and pull myself over to it. Climbing the ladder to this boxcar's little steel platform on top where the car's "manual" brake wheel was located allowed me to hang onto the wheel with my arm thrust through it… with my bottom on the tiny platform. By now the train had settled at a high speed and, with my upper body above the boxcar top, the strong wind was giving me a pounding. To lose my grip on the small brake wheel would be instant death…because that would mean falling straight down onto the track between the thundering cars.

It was so dangerous that I slowly took off my belt and threaded it through one of the little wheel's spokes…then through about half of my belt loops and "bear-hugged" the wheel. Hanging on for dear life as the wind blasted me, the gondola I escaped from still pounded away like a jackhammer.

For over sixty miles the train held its speed. Each time it seemed almost impossible to continue holding, the vision of deadly track rushing by below forced me to tighten my weary grip knowing that losing that grip—a gloomy thought—likely would cause my belt to break and drop me to crushing doom.

Finally, the train slowed and ultimately stopped on a siding so another train could pass! Never having had any experience even close to this desperate situation, my body literally shook with fright for a long time after bailing off that infernal machine.

Be guaranteed that the few more times in my young life when

"freight-train-hopping," checking thoroughly for "flat wheels" was first priority!

It was pure pleasure to get back on the good old curvy and romantic Columbia Highway and "thumb" it home. Sharp curves never looked so good!

A modern "container" train cruises the same rails as the one in my "flat wheel" incident.

View east from Rowena Crest Viewpoint

Author at age 13+
...a good year for hitchhiking
and freight-train hopping

Try to picture two giant trucks with long trailers passing on this curve. The precarious road could either "make" or "break" a truck driver.

The earliest trucks on the old Columbia River Highway were "open air" affairs.

During my days of "hitchhiking," the old road was only slightly better than this early photo illustration.

In the 1940s and 50s, Freightliner "tractors" like these pulled many of the biggest loads over the old highway.

An auto equipment ad of 1920. This is the type of traffic one could expect in the early days of the old highway. The possibility of meeting oncoming autos in the middle of a narrow sharp curve or switchback posed significant danger.

In the 1930s, autos on the old highway became more powerful.

Hood River Valley along the old historic highway
- Photo circa 1931 -

In 1928, Oregon's premier airplane pilot, "Tex" Rankin, declared the Columbia Gorge a superb route for airliners to sneak upriver under clouds. Imagine looking down from Vista House through fog to see an airliner flying...*beneath you!*

Crashing over a guardrail was not advisable on the old highway.

Cold Shoulders

In 1950, a cousin and his family came from Minnesota to visit us. Three things were memorable from that visit.

First, he wore "Stradivari" shirts which were so classy that, when finally making enough money, I bought some for myself. Good move…they really impressed the girls.

Of the other two remembrances, the first was of him at the piano playing the Johann Strauss composition, "Voices of Spring," a song that strongly impressed me and delights me to this day. The other memory: we two came within a "frog-hair" of losing his dad's pristine-condition car over an almost vertical drop-off at the edge of…you guessed it…the historic old *Columbia River Highway!*

It happened in the early spring when northwestern Oregon is well known for being damp and mushy because the soil still holds much moisture from the long winter of rain.

We cousins were enthusiastic hunters. We were not alone. A significant percentage of the population was quite familiar with guns and fishing poles. In the middle of the twentieth century, Oregon's highways leading to deer and elk hunting areas were as crowded with excited hunters during hunting season as they are now with people driving to their vacation homes. Hunting was completely acceptable…a major activity in the lives of many. As late as the 1960s, deer and gamebird hunting in Oregon were still considered good sports that also helped put some meat on the table.

Jim and I wanted to brush up on our shooting skills and one way to do that was crow shooting. Crows were considered pests which

Gorge crow hunting expedition

could decimate some types of crops and that was the justification for eliminating them. Numerous crows nested near the railroad tracks running along the old highway. We headed there in Jim's dad's car.

Driving west a few hundred yards past the settlement of Bridal Veil, we spotted some crows on our right and Jim instantly whipped over to a roadside halt.

When the old highway was built, there was little traffic and wide roads were not required. It also cost a ton of money to build wide roads due to relatively primitive equipment. The result: extremely narrow road "shoulders" at many places along the old highway. Extremely? How about almost *nonexistent* in many places! And...*Jim had attempted to park on one of these places!*

Popping the door open, I jumped out on the right...and immediately dropped down about twenty-five feet until stopped against a tree. It wasn't a vertical drop, but exceedingly steep. The shoulder was so narrow and Jim had pulled over so far that there just was *no shoulder left*. Hurtling down didn't bother me but it became obvious the car was beginning to tip over toward me as it squeezed slowly down into soft rain-soaked, oozy shoulder/earth. Yelling to Jim at the top of my lungs, I told him to grab the car by a door handle and attempt to hold it allowing me to get away before it could roll over and crash down on me.

When he figured out what the yelling was about...he did as requested and held fast to the car. It was that close! He actually held the car with just a modest amount of effort and barely kept it from rolling over the steep drop to smashed-up oblivion...and smashed-up ME!

To escape this bizarre development, I climbed up and switched holds with him...and held the car in that position for over an hour as he rushed about the settlement of Bridal Veil looking for help to remove the car from the dangerous shoulder. Luckily, he found a tow truck in time to hook onto the car and save it from crashing over the steep bank. That ended our day of crow hunting.

Because of that unique incident, I continue to be wary of the narrow and soft "shoulders" along the old highway. Driving it today is *still dangerous!* Every time I drive it, checking that same spot where we had that quirky experience reveals that nothing has changed and yes, there it is...the same treacherous foot-wide shoulder.

Concrete milepost on the old highway...this one is located on the hiking/biking trail between Hood River and Mosier.

While skinny shoulders of the old road that almost claimed our car are still a hazard, improving them to modern roadway standards certainly would diminish the beauty of one of the most scenic drives in America.

Looking east from Vista House...
Visitors are captivated by this magnificent view.

Sleeping trailers like this were a common
sight on the early highway.

Along "Twin Tunnels" hiking/biking trail

One of many interesting stops along the legendary old
highway...located in historic Mosier between
Hood River and The Dalles

Photo taken upon completion of "Rowena Loops"

Looped

Harry was an exceptionally nice fellow who was about eight years older than I. Large for my age, I always tried to act much older and, truth be told, it was occasionally for purposes of buying beer. My older appearance probably eased any concerns Harry might have had about my younger age. At any rate, we hit it off as friends right away.

Harry was an extremely dedicated and hard worker. He worked in a cold storage room removing cartons of milk bottles from a constantly moving conveyor...all day long. It was hard to understand how anyone could work very long at such a job…but he did and did it well. The job may have lacked inspiration, but not for Harry. He had another commendable attribute: *he saved his money!* That made it possible for Harry to buy a new car...right off the showroom floor!

The new car helped considerably in the quest for female friendship. Don't know why it is but girls just seemed to go for guys with late model cars. Wonder if that has changed any?

One night we had only ourselves for company. We hit a few taverns and had a few beers…then took a break to discuss our next move. It was getting late and we were still in control of what we judged a major measure of our reasoning and motor-control powers. As there were no girls in sight, we decided to effect a significant change of scenery. This was a Friday night in late fall and the famed Pendleton Roundup was in full swing. We decided to head for the Roundup…*immediately!*

It was about midnight when this momentous plan engaged our

Mosier Creek bridge on the old highway

thoughts. Sooo…away we went in Harry's brand-new Chevrolet! From Troutdale to Pendleton…a couple of hundred miles!

We drove the old highway and, at Hood River, Harry decided he was too sleepy and dragged-out to continue driving…and asked if I would like to take over?

Would I take over? Hey…this was a brand new car! Few young people had new cars. Such a privilege was rare.

"Yeah"…I said instantly, "Sure…I'll drive."

We rolled out of Hood River and up the first set of switchbacks at the edge of town. The sweet-smelling new auto hummed along smoothly.

Wheeling through the old town of Mosier and up into the hills beyond, we passed cherry orchards like those still cultivated there today. Then the historic "Mayer" home came into view. It is one of the grandest structures on the entire stretch of the old Columbia River Highway.

Harry had gone to sleep by this time and we were really covering ground…and I was having a grand time at the wheel! We headed down the first stretch of the ill-famed "Rowena Loops" and it was necessary to cut the throttle back a little. All was going smoothly and my semi-race-driver technique was working beautifully. It was indeed thrilling to be the driver.

Hitting the first major loop, we rolled around it with no problem. By the second big loop, we were moving fast enough for the tires to squeal a little…but not enough to wake Harry. Neatly twisting the steering wheel to negotiate the sharp curve…it suddenly appeared as if the road had changed in color from normal asphalt gray to jet-black! Strange!

Unfortunately, there was only a micro-second to mull this over and the car went into a sickening skid on…*black ice!*

Water "runoff" had found its way over that section of highway, had completely covered it for a length of a hundred feet or so…and had frozen solid!

"Locals" probably knew of this nasty hazard and how to approach it…but we were a long way from being local.

In my defense…at least we weren't going a zillion miles an hour. My speed was actually down a little from what it might have been had the auto been mine.

That didn't make much difference. The "black ice" caused the car to go into an uncontrolled slide and neatly take out the guardrail. Well…in a manner of speaking. It didn't actually remove any of the guardrail but the guardrail did remove some parts of the car. The crash mashed the grill in and jimmied up the front of the hood. I cringe a little to tell this…but the car probably received a good three hundred dollars worth of damage (converted to present values…about three thousand or so).

"Chagrined" is not a strong enough word to describe how I felt: ashamed of myself, mad at myself and sad about what had been done to Harry's beautiful car plus a number of other feelings of guilt. However…the deed was done! The brand new car was "smushed"…in major ways.

Of course, Harry came to with a start. Then he got out quietly… walked to the front of the car…and shook his head in disbelief. How could this happen to a two-week-old brand new car?

Harry deserved a monumental amount of credit. Had our positions

95

been reversed, he might not have been as lucky. What I remember most is…he didn't kill me on the spot!

My immediate response was to mumble in high gear about accepting full responsibility for the damage and paying the fifty-dollar deductible insurance bill right away (an entire week's paycheck at the time). Mortified by my act, that was all I could think of to say.

A half hour or so of checking the car over proved it to be perfectly drivable so we powwowed over our next move. After some discussion, we decided what the heck… we'd gone this far…might as well carry on and go all the way to Pendleton. So…we jammed the smashed hood down on its bent holder and, with Harry now at the wheel (that figures), we continued (not quite merrily) on our way.

Viewing Pendleton Roundup action was our goal.

In all the time we spent ruefully viewing our damage, talking the situation over and making sure the car was drivable, not one car or truck passed us. That's how little traffic there was.

Back on the road, we drove on to The Dalles and stopped for coffee to calm down a bit. Harry was an absolute white knight about what had just been done! That made me all the more embarrassed. What bothered me most was the fact that it really wasn't crazy driving on my part that caused the crash. It was just lack of experience in clearly understanding "black ice" conditions. Nonetheless, I had done a yeoman's job of wrecking his nice new jewel and it disturbed me to the core. Finishing our coffee, we got back in the car and moved out.

Most of the old Columbia River Highway was still in its original configuration at the time…with a couple of exceptions. The new "water level route" (which would become "I-84" in future years) was under construction for a distance beyond The Dalles. We hit it doing around

Author as 16-year-old truck driver...had much better luck with truck than with friend Harry's new car.

sixty or so and, although it was still just graded gravel, it was smooth and straight sailing. Sooo…Harry pushed the accelerator down a bit further. Big mistake!

The lights went out!

Nooo…not the headlights! All forward vision!

"What happened?" we yelled in unison.

"Hold it straight, Harry," I shouted!

We couldn't see a thing! Forward visibility was zero!

It took a few very nervous seconds to figure it out while still rolling at high speed. Then it became clear. The hood had broken loose from its damaged hold-down! And that wasn't the half of it!

The hood had come loose and the wind had whipped it up with what seemed the speed of a lightning bolt…then smashed it into the windshield in the flick of an eyelash!

The only good news was zero traffic on the road and the fact that Harry was able to guide the car swervingly to a stop...without *another* crash.

Finally stopped, we both sat still as statues while we gathered our senses from the shock of this new catastrophic attack of fate on Harry's

View from "Twin tunnels" trail on the old highway.

pride and joy. Jeeezz…would it never end?

Checking the car over, after the second major disaster in less than an hour, the results of our inspection proved even more disheartening than the first. The loose hood had flown up with such force that it shoved both doorframes back from the window column posts…far enough that now we couldn't completely close either front door.

Son-of-a-gun! Talk about bad news! We had to wire the doors shut.

Now I was beyond a total loss for words! It was entirely my fault. Harry just stared at the carnage. It was almost too much!

That ended our opportunity to see the Pendleton Roundup. I've never been as close to visiting it again. We turned around…and drove silently home.

It's been a lot of years since that calamitous debacle on the "Rowena Loops" of the renowned old Columbia River highway.

Wherever you are Harry…*please forgive me.*

The Rowena Loop that did me in with... "*black ice!*"

Map labels:
COLUMBIA RIVER

EXIT 69

84

84 EXIT 64

HOOD
RIVER

Mark O. Hatfield
TRAILHEAD WEST

PARKING

HISTORIC COLUMBIA RIVER HWY STATE TRAIL

MOSIER
TWIN
TUNNELS

MOSIER

Mark O. Hatfield
TRAILHEAD EAST

PARKING

ROCK CREEK RD

35

TO MT. HOOD

HOOD RIVER

N

I-84
HCRH (Driveable)
HCRH (Hikeable)
OTHER ROADS
RAILROAD

Twin Tunnels hiking/biking trail

This map illustrates the trail through "Twin Tunnels" on a closed section of the old highway between Hood River and The Dalles. The trail and work on the tunnels were sizable undertakings accomplished by the Oregon State Highway Department to make this stretch of the original highway accessible to the public. Although the scenery is spectacular, the trail indicated from the Hood River end to the tunnels is not for the faint-hearted. It is about four miles long with numerous ups and downs. The trail from the Mosier end to the tunnels is shorter but a much steeper grade for the distance traveled. The trail offers some of the most beautiful views in the entire state and a hike or bike ride on it is an exhilarating experience.

100

Viewpoint on Twin Tunnels hiking/biking trail near Mosier

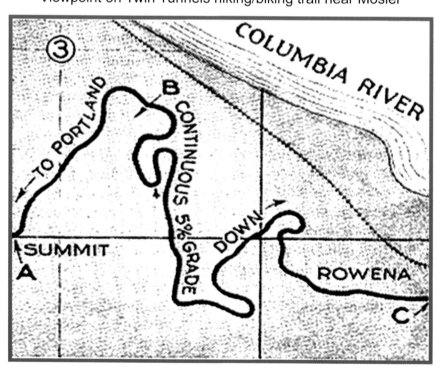

1923 map illustrating details of the new "Rowena Loops"

A wary creature

Honk If You're A Honker

Putting a wild goose on the family's dinner table at Christmas was always one of my heart's desires especially since we are Danish and historic Danish tradition is serving goose at Christmas time. My dad was a devout sportsman and hunter and exposed me to the outdoor world from earliest childhood. Dad's hunting experiences taught me how difficult it can be to "bring home the bacon" in the form of a goose. He seldom came home with these wily creatures in his game bag but not for lack of trying. Most "shootable" geese in northern Oregon gather to feed on private grain fields on hills above the Columbia River and, if you don't have the right connections with farmers, you are hard-pressed to do much productive goose shooting. Thus, my dad would have to try his luck at public shooting grounds…usually with mediocre results.

There was a time when Dad's work would be bypassed in a flash for the opportunity to go shot-gunning for game birds. Of the different game birds available, the Canadian Honker was one of the most difficult to capture. However, one time in my life I managed to bag a Honker. It thrilled me! It may not sound like much but, in the world of waterfowl hunters, it was a small but notable milestone.

After the goose was shot, it didn't drop but faltered, set its wings and sailed over water-filled irrigation ditches and levees for a mile or so. It took from afternoon into darkness to traverse all that miserable terrain to find the bird…dead in thigh-high wheat stubble in a field a mile square. This on the second and last day of the hunt.

That was my only success with goose hunting. After the hunt, I drove 300 miles home to my bachelor apartment to find in my mail a "Greetings from your Uncle Sam" mandatory invitation to join the U.S. Army! You can bet the exact date of that goose hunt is well remembered.

The old-timers on that trip taught me a lot about the lore of geese and, from that day to this my respect has been high for the majestic Canadian "Honker" goose. Although not too successful hunting geese, my experiences with them did qualify me to know a fair amount about them.

Before the Columbia River was dammed completely from source to mouth, big Canadian geese accumulated by the millions along the upper river shores. In later years, after learning to fly and buying a small Piper "Cub" plane, I found it interesting to cruise along the spectacular Columbia Gorge observing smaller flocks…much diminished as a result of the multiple dam construction.

On one occasion, a few hours of time away from business to "cut holes in the sky" found me flying my little J3-85 Piper Cub above the river. Approaching Vista House, unusual objects appeared in the air directly in front about a half mile out and below my altitude a hundred feet or so. Typically, all one sees from a slow private plane are seagulls, crows and an occasional hawk or buzzard.

Drawing closer, it became apparent these were very big geese. No question about it…they were "*Canadian Honkers.*" They appeared to be in one large "Vee" formation of sixty or seventy birds. Unbelievable! I had never imagined that a small plane would come this close to geese in midair. There is no way a non-hunter can comprehend the fires of sub-conscious desire such a confrontation will produce within the hammering heart of a "hunter-gatherer."

I aimed for the flock!

In the heat of the moment, it didn't immediately register in my goose-addled brain that I wasn't hunting, didn't have a gun and was locked in an airplane at two thousand feet. If that wasn't enough, approaching was an inhabited area probably running over with sensitive bird-watcher types in plain sight…and flying near birds would be harassing wildlife, something that in modern times can cost you money, your airplane and maybe some time in the pokey.

To the side went my left hand…to jam the little round red-knob throttle lever forward with gusto. I decided to be a bit whacko and try flying formation with them. Amazing what people will do in moments of insane less-than-clearly-considered zeal. In a warped hot-pursuit way of thinking, these babies were fair game for major sport. Hey, we were sharing the same airspace and we all had wings so why couldn't we fly together for a while?

The plane closed in on them!

Have you ever thought about what or how birds in the sky actually operate? They always seem to be up there just doing their thing. But they really are feathered flying machines with a semblance of a brain and the accompanying ability to think, see, reason and react to assorted circumstances when it might directly affect their welfare. It was soon obvious that birds are pretty sharp indeed when threatened.

The closer the plane got, the bigger they appeared. It was surprising to realize that the plane was actually flying right up behind them with relative ease. In sneaking up on ordinary birds such as crows or ravens, the tiniest hint of moving the airplane toward them would cause them to dive and disappear. These geese just held their formation like a flight of air force cadets fearful of crashing if they moved out position by one inch. Outstanding discipline! They just held their positions…no matter what.

One thing became obvious immediately. Approaching close enough to see their distinct features, a couple of them were looking back over their shoulders (they have shoulders?) at this giant noisy foreign dragonfly…with clearly evident concern. We were rapidly coming eyeball to eyeball. Their concern seemed to be highly controlled and they appeared to be talking to each other and discussing the situation as if contemplating what actions they should take to eliminate this threat.

Flying close, I eased back on the throttle and transitioned to slow-flight mode behind them.

They speeded up to stay ahead.

We evened out at the same airspeed, approximately forty miles an hour in level flight. The plane could go a bit slower but not much without

105

My plane approached the flight of geese near Vista House.

With little hunting pressure, "Honkers" have made themselves
quite at home year round in the Gorge.

We hunted ducks and geese on Columbia islands

Old hunters are amazed to see big honkers now unafraid of humans. Just goes to show how far society has moved from "hunting & gathering"...to quickie hamburgers and pizza!

107

falling out of the sky. Maybe they could have gone faster but probably not without having bird heart attacks. It seemed they had "fire-walled" their briskly flapping wings and were flying as fast as they could.

We stayed even.

The group, holding formation, must have taken an order from whichever was the bird "squadron leader" because, as soon as they decided they couldn't outrun the plane, they initiated an evasive maneuver to dive and turn away. Their move was in absolute unison and smooth as silk. These fellows were masters of the sky and they didn't waste a lot of fuel doing nutty things like airplane pilots do. They continued to hold formation as if they were all glued in place and made every move count. Impressive! Could we somehow domesticate this group? In their spare time, we might get them to teach Blue Angel flight candidates.

The plane dived and turned with them.

They pulled up and executed a climbing turn.

The plane followed.

They abruptly dived.

Down went the plane!

They set their wings for a glide.

The plane stayed right on their tails.

The entire proceeding was bizarre! Flying formation with a flock of geese! A fascinating part was that the geese seemed almost human as, one by one, they turned their heads back and coolly looked me over. It was as if they were carefully gauging my airspeed and, with that information, considering their next evasive maneuver. No serious panic here...only group resolve to maintain an unwavering discipline. Here were magnificent birds worthy of much respect.

Now...if you are an Audubon-type person, please know that no birds were injured in this aerial flirtation and all of them most likely lived happily ever after. And, hey, I could have been out instead in a hunting blind somewhere...sneakily waiting for these same birds to come down to be blasted with my shotgun!

You might think the story should end here. But *it didn't.*

As my interest in the activity began to wane, one goose appeared to be running out of gas. He broke formation, set his wings and began a long descending glide down and away from his flying buddies.

It just didn't seem right to let that "lone ranger" go without following him down and it surprised me how easily the Cub maneuvered sharply enough to stay right with him.

He moved right.

The plane moved right.

He pulled up.

The plane pulled up.

It was eerie.

This bird "goose-plane" was made of bones, flesh and feathers and yet it was flying just like a real airplane. It was as if the two of us were now flying "wingman" formation and he was going like a bullet! We were doing around sixty or more on the way down. He gave up trying to beat his wings to hold or increase altitude. He just continued gliding down. It looked like he was running on empty...a simple matter of time until he had to do something rash.

While mulling this over, a jolt of unpleasant awareness struck me that, not only had we descended to a low altitude, we now were rapidly approaching the center of the suburban village of Gresham. Engrossed in my aerial nature studies, I'd failed to pay adequate attention to my position. Now my situation became nervous. It was possible some real bird watchers might accidentally glance up at the sky and see us flying together. It might appear to some as if a giant motorized hawk was bearing down on a poor defenseless bird...a bird of which children's nursery rhymes are made.

Then, facing the possibility of someone reading my aircraft number and calling the bird police, I beat a quick retreat by banking sharply and hustling the heck "out of Dodge."

While pondering the potential outcome in the event someone did get my number and reported me, worry now occupied my thoughts. Cruising along, I mulled over the potential consequences of my indiscretion.

What would be my plea? "Temporary insanity?"

Ah, well... it had been a blast and no wildlife had been injured so what the heck!

My nervousness increased during the swift return to home base...and getting down and out of the plane pronto was my earnest desire (as if that might somehow reduce my exposure to discovery, punishment and shame).

The government requires giant one-foot high registration numbers in plain sight on the sides of planes. Not pretty! Why didn't I think about the number exposure up there when it counted and either forget the damn geese or at least try to hold the plane in a configuration that would make the numbers difficult to see?

A couple of days went by and I was a recovered man.

Hadn't heard a thing from the FAA, the FBI, the CIA, YMCA, DAR or the Audubon Society. Apparently, a clean getaway had been made. Amazing the feeling of relief that produces!

A few more days went by and this incident had been assigned to ancient history when one local morning newspaper featured an interesting story and a big photograph.

Unbelievable!

There…as big as life and snapped not far from where my plane had left the lone bird…was a photo of a homeowner standing in his front yard feeding a giant Canadian "Honker" goose.

He told a story about the wild goose arriving in his yard a couple of days earlier…apparently all worn out from its flight south. The goose was friendly and seemed to want nothing more than to stay in his yard, rest and eat. The man had been feeding the bird hoping to see it get up enough steam to continue its way south. He just couldn't understand why it wasn't in any hurry to leave.

If you are wondering? Noooo…I didn't call the man (or anybody else for that matter) to inquire or talk about it. No sir, I was content to simply read about it in the paper like three or four hundred thousand other people and be just as bemused as they were!

The plane I flew with Canadian Honker "formation"

This little Piper Cub that served me well on many adventurous excursions. Its short field capabilities made it possible for me to hunt pheasants on a small island in the middle of the Columbia River only a few hundred yards from Portland International Airport. On one outing, an island just east of Vista House beckoned. To prove the little ship's short-field performance (*and* amaze nearby waterskiers), attempting a landing on a very narrow stretch of beach seemed an exciting thing to do. The landing came off perfectly but, upon deplaning, it was my own surprise to realize the plane's wheels were sinking fast in soft oozy mud-sand. It seems I had miscalculated the solidity of the earth...and it was only by much rapid gut-busting hustling that it was possible to search out a couple of planks, jack the plane up onto them...and make an extremely close-shave takeoff before the plane sank beyond recovery.

Other sport was to fly up the Columbia on days when the wind was blowing down the Gorge at more than thirty-five miles an hour. The plane had the ability to "slow-fly" at speeds as low as thirty miles an hour by holding power and increasing the plane's "attitude." In strong wind, I would fly up close to Vista House...then move the ship over until it was level and even with the sidewalk. Slowly easing the throttle back, the plane in slow-flight would settle into what appeared to be absolute dead-still suspended animation in the sky. The high wind and the plane's slow-speed matched and the plane could stay in place as if hanging from a sky-hook. Amazed tourists would rush over to the wall to observe in awe! Doing this today probably would net me an instantly-suspended pilot's license.

The Columbia River Highway as it was in 1931.

View from Twin Tunnels hiking/biking trail

Early autos were operated like modern-day SUVs until roads like the Columbia River Highway made smoother travel possible.

Columbia River Highway drivers were thrilled when they could escape strong Gorge east winds in an enclosed car.

The grand
Columbia Gorge Hotel

Memorial bronze honoring Simon Benson...lumberman, philanthropist, builder of Columbia Gorge Hotel and sponsor of historic Columbia River Highway.

Bronze is located at Multnomah Falls.

Lessons in finance at the Columbia Gorge Hotel

In the early nineteen-eighties, my involvement in a scheme to dazzle a person with one of the more flashy birthday parties ever… served to give me a sound education.

A debt of gratitude was owed the birthday person for many generous kindnesses given and it was decided this party should be the "big one." After assembling a group of thirty or so friends, a large bus was hired along with a three-piece German "Oompah" band and an on-board bartender to serve enroute. The participants all agreed to share the expenses equally.

At twilight, we left Portland for the beautifully restored Columbia Gorge Hotel on the old Columbia River Highway west of the city of Hood River. We sang and "libated" our way to the "grand old dame" of the Gorge and arrived in fine spirits.

Earlier, I had driven to Hood River to make arrangements and visited the high school. There, a couple of uniformed trumpet players were engaged to stand on each side of the bus door and sound a "fanfare" upon our arrival at the hotel. A pretty piano player from the city agreed to tap piano keys and sing for us during the long evening and a visit to a local winery confirmed that native wine would be delivered ahead to the hotel for the soiree.

The trumpet fanfare kids were right on time and amazed everyone. The birthday event took place in a large room adjoining the

One of numerous spectacular waterfalls along the old highway

dining room and came off beautifully. The piano gal played until the "last dog was hung." The food was excellent and the hotel catered to our every whim. Lifetime memories were made! Outstanding! We rode home as a happy group of merrymakers…serenaded all the way by the now thoroughly-bored band.

One more of life's major lessons was learned from this undertaking which had required many days to assemble. It was…*beware of promises made in the heat of enthusiasm.* The illusion that all the people who wished to be a part of the big surprise had enough money (and the good intentions) to pay up *pronto*…proved to be just that. To expedite the proceedings, it had been necessary that I front a sizable amount of money for a number of the group and, when trying to collect later, one of the biggest debtors tried to stiff me. Like *five hundred bucks worth!* Not wanting to get burned for that amount, I hung in like a burr and, after a few months of hounding, the slacker finally coughed up.

You've heard the old admonishment, "*Get it in writing?*" Well…here's another for you…

"Get the cash in your hot hands…***first!***"

A view from Columbia Gorge Hotel...
Hundreds of wind-surfers ride the waters on a windy day.

The dry Rowena Plateau

Rowena Crest Viewpoint from "Loops" below

The outstanding old Mayer mansion near Rowena loops
(while undergoing a "facelift")

Mayer Mansion

First riding past the Mayer mansion as a young hitchhiker, then driving by much later as an automobile owner, a commanding "twinge" of hard-core envy and nostalgia would sweep over me...envy "just because" and nostalgia dreaming about earlier romantic times.

The Mayer home is one of a few true "mansions" on the entire stretch of highway. According to one written history, the orchards and other crops were planted on the property around 1910 when "Markie" Mayer arrived in the area. The house was completed by him about the time the highway was begun in 1913. The property apparently has been an orchard operation from the beginning and is still planted in large cherry orchards. When I passed it as a "hitchhiker" in the 1940s and 50s (six times just from age 13 to 15), it was a wonder to me that people could afford such classy homes and giant acreages.

Much later...and surprisingly, I would become a welcomed guest in the interesting old Mayer house. In the 1960s, a family member was acquainted with people living there. We were invited to visit and jumped at the chance. The home was as intriguing and imposing inside as it appeared from the highway and we enjoyed "tea" with the occupants. They told us the old Mayer Building in Portland was a part of the early homeowner's family business interests.

The old "Mayer" estate...known almost from the beginning as "Mayerdale," is an outstanding sight on the old highway...and deserves a good look while passing by.

Columbia Gorge near the Mayer property

The new world of super-overkill
(3 giants on one small boat)

HorsePOWER

(on the Columbia River)

While visiting a Columbia River dock, a boat about 25 feet long caught my attention...and my eyeballs fairly popped in amazement. The boat was "outboard" powered and this baby was *unusual!*

It had 3 (three) outboard motors and they were big. No...not big...*gigantic!* 225 horsepower each! On one relatively small boat! Add it up...that's 675 HP on the tail-end of a boat of the type that used to have much the same (or a bit less) horsepower than a Roman chariot.

How's your arithmetic? Fairly good? Then try this. How much is the sum of three 225-horse outboard motors at *sixteen thousand* bucks each? Think you got the answer? Nope...that's not it. The answer is...three times more than was paid for my first 3-bedroom, 2-bath house! Yeahhh...we all know about "changing times" and, yeah, I'm an old geezer and you've heard it all before...but this was ridiculous! 675 horsepower to run just one modestly-sized boat? You know what I think? 225+225+225=*insanity plus!*

During WWII, Dad worked in Oregon shipyards. When the war was over, he was ready to get back to fishing.

He needed an outboard motor and, because the war had limited all non-essential manufacturing, no new motors were to be had. That didn't stop him! We lived near the Columbia River and it was chock full of salmon in the late summer and early fall. He couldn't wait to go after them.

The very first postwar year, Dad got his name in line with a local boat builder for a new plywood "skiff." His order was for a sixteen-footer…a "bottom-of-the-line" boat…actually, a glorified rowboat. He converted an old two-wheel cargo trailer into a boat trailer to haul it.

While the boat was being built, he searched fruitlessly for a used outboard motor. Still, no new outboards were yet available. Fishing guys were hoarding that kind of stuff because of a tremendous scarcity. It would be another two to three years before new outboard motors would become readily available. Dad couldn't wait! He continued searching and finally got lucky when a widow sold him her deceased husband's outboard motor.

The motor was a 1939 Johnson two and a half horse. Yep! Two and a half! That's "2 ½!"…only *two and a half horsepower!* You following this?

It was the famous Johnson "Seahorse" motor…a cute little "pee-wee" that you had to start by pulling a separate rope. The rope went around the flywheel located right on top of the motor. A neat feature of this little gem was its light weight. Full of gas, it checked in at about thirty-five pounds. Of course, two and a half horse won't even make the grade as a trolling motor today but back then it was surprising what jobs these little babies were asked to do.

Dad was lucky and had to pay only a small fortune to the widow. Her husband may have just gone to that big fishing hole in the sky, but she surely knew that everybody and his brother was hot for his motor.

The legendary Chinook salmon in the massive Columbia River at the head of the Columbia Gorge were my dad's target. The river is well known for it's fast current downstream from the last dam and that's where we fished. We usually anchored in a "hog-line" on one of the faster sections of the river! What's a "hog-line? It's where a whole bunch of boats anchor side by side in a line straight across the river. They are so close they have to have boat bumpers on each side to keep from rubbing. If the fishing was good, there would sometimes be thirty or forty boats in a line.

Dad was pretty slick when it came to water and fishing. He had been around the woods and water all his life. He knew little tricks old Neptune would have been happy to learn. Regarding Dad's little outboard, most of you "boatmen" are probably thinking that a little "two and a half" couldn't possibly make "headway" against the eight or ten mile-an-hour current of the mighty Columbia. Heck…*any fool knows that!*

When we put the boat in the water, we didn't just charge right out into the middle of the stream like a couple of nitwit amateurs. *Of course not!* At the time, most of the other fishermen had bigger motors…like five-horse…and a few even had sevens and tens. *Not us!* So Dad simply hugged the bank where friction slows the water. In the friction-slowed near-the-bank water, we could make just enough headway upriver to reach the Sandy River's mouth where it empties into the Columbia…about a half-mile above where the hog-line of fishing boats was anchored in the middle of the fastest water. Then dad would aim the boat diagonally out toward the river center in a forty-five degree "tack" and, as we lost ground against the strong current, the tack would carry us right over to the hog-line. We then pitched the anchor out, dropped into a slot between boats and proceeded to fish our hearts out. Clever Dad!…and *that* with just *two and a half horsepower!*

There was one major potential drawback to this quaint operation. If we missed the hole in the hog-line…there wouldn't be enough time to make a second go-around to try dropping into it again so we would have to give up and go home.

Thus….a few words for "*over-horsed*" characters with giant motors who might be a little short on boating abilities. Next time you go out on fast water with those monumental wave-makers, *throttle back six hundred seventy-two and half horses*…and then find out how really handy you are with a boat!